WHEN LIBERTY

ENSLAVES

The Toxic Blend of Faith and Politics

JERRY AVETA

For information, contact

MSI Press, LLC
1760-F Airline Hwy #203
Hollister, CA 95023

Copyeditor: Betty Lou Leaver
Cover Design & Layout: Opeyemi Ikuborije

ISBN: 978-1-957354-50-7

Library of Congress Control Number: 2024915848

Epigraph

"The true rule, in determining to embrace or reject anything, is not whether it have *any* evil in it; but whether it have more of evil than of good. There are few things *wholly* evil, or *wholly* good. Almost everything, especially of governmental policy, is an inseparable compound of the two; so that our best judgment of the preponderance between them is continually demanded."

Abraham Lincoln, 1848

CONTENTS

PART 3 WHEN LIBERTY ENSLAVES: LET FREEDOM RING

Introduction

I have never been an avid student of history. My only interest in the subject was when a specific history course was required to attain a diploma or a degree. The type of history didn't matter. I was not interested. Engineering students like me looked at those studying history with disdain. We referred to the football stadium as "L.A. Beach." That is where the "Liberal Arts" students, like those studying history, spent their spring afternoons sunbathing while we labored through our various engineering labs.

This lack of interest was the result of my classroom experiences, in which the teachers' lectures blurred into a series of indistinguishable words and inaudible sounds that made no sense to me at all. When it came time to study for a test, all I found in my notes were a series of random entries of dates and names surrounded by pages of doodles. Needless to say, I did not excel in these studies. I was elated if I escaped each course with a passing grade.

Because of this experience, my mind was closed, and my attitude was negative concerning the subject. As a matter of practical experience, I failed to realize the social and moral implications that often are affected by historical events. That is, until recently. While reading about the state of our union leading up to the Civil War, I was deeply moved by the similarities between those conditions and those present in our nation today. The parallels between then and now are stark and sobering. Stark in that opposing views concerning the social issues of the time permeated the nation. Sobering in the realization that these conditions were easily promoted to provoke civil conflict and eventually war. This realization has produced a deep regret for my having ignored the value of history for most of my life. But more important, it has increased my concern dramatically that our nation is living through a perilous time.

Comparing the pre-Civil War days to now, I find a common experience. Both times contain a nexus between faith and politics, a linkage that causes twists and turns in the way our nation is governed to conform to these polarizing influences. In times past, there was a common understanding never to mix politics and religion in the same conversation. However, today discussions of politics and faith routinely fill social media. The combination of the two has been extensively analyzed as influential in the outcomes of recent elections. During the times leading up to the Civil War, this same confluence of faith and politics can be found in the election process and the governing of our nation. From the reading of those past events and living through the current times, we learn the reason for the warning never to mix faith and politics in our social discourse. Their intersection results in a toxic social environment that is taxing to normal relationships, relationships that often become short in conversation and high in emotion. This bears true then and now.

An autopsy of the pre-Civil War and our times reveals different social issues colliding with the faith of these times. Although the social issues differ, they resemble how each vexes the heart and penetrates the soul of our society. At the core of the matter lie issues of life and death. Both experiences offer choices of liberty or enslavement.

During the Civil War era, the exercise of liberty in our nation centered on the issue of equality. Some believed all men were created equal with equal rights. Some believed all men were not created equal and did not have equal rights. At that time, people of the same faith were found on both sides of these issues.

About our experience today, the exercise of liberty in our nation concerns the sanctity of life. Some believe the sanctity of life includes guaranteeing the birth of every fetus, regardless of the circumstances of the pregnancy. Some people believe the sanctity of life includes the liberty to manage the development of the fetus, maximizing the general welfare of both mother and child. Here too, people of the same faith are found on both sides of the issue.

Also, in our experience today, some people believe the sanctity of life includes constraints in the use of guns and the elimination of automatic weapons. Some people believe liberty includes the right to stockpile ammunition and weapons without any constraint. Once again, we find people of the same faith on both sides of this issue.

The social issues of today differ from each other and even more so from those of years ago, but all are emotional and powerful enough to already have caused a divide in our nation. The only unknown is to what extent these issues will further divide. Can they be so divisive that for the second time in our history, Americans will take up arms against one another? That is yet to be determined, but we can learn from history and the examples of some great leaders during those times.

On June 16, 1858, the Illinois Republican Convention nominated Abraham Lincoln as their candidate for the U.S. Senate. In his acceptance speech for that nomination, Lincoln stated that a divided nation would not stay divided. It would become either entirely free or a slave nation. I would suggest the same is true for our nation today. We will become a nation that continues to remain free in our liberty or continue to restrict our liberties more and more.

Our nation's divisions have grown in part due to recent Supreme Court decisions reversing what many in our nation believe to be a constitutional right protecting the general welfare of a woman's body. Many now feel enslaved because faith has been used to fuel a political outcome that has reversed the freedom that existed for generations in our nation. They feel enslaved by the "liberty" of others, including others of the same faith.

Additionally, our nation's divide has been accelerated because legislators refuse to adopt any restrictions on gun access and their use. Many in our nation feel subjected to violence while routinely shopping in the mall, attending worship services, enjoying outdoor concerts, or attending school. Here again, many in our nation feel enslaved by this violence because of the "liberty" of others.

This phenomenon of "one person's liberty enslaving another" is not unique to our times. It existed during the days of Lincoln as well. Frederick Douglas had been born into enslavement in the state of Maryland in 1818. Having escaped to freedom, he became a widely published author and editor of *The North Star* a Rochester, New York newspaper. Addressing a crowd on July 4, 1872, Douglas stated the following: "*The sunlight that brought life and healing to you, has brought stripes and death to me. The Fourth of July is yours, not mine. You may rejoice, I must mourn.*"[1] What was one people's "liberty" was causing the enslavement of others.

"Feeling" enslaved is quite different from "being" enslaved and in that regard, our times are blessedly different from the pre-Civil War days. But these two times in our nation's history are decidedly similar, bending faith to conform to politics to justify their preferred outcome.

Slavery is racism in its purest form. While our nation has been purged of slavery, racism remains. The depths and the extent of racism that we see in our country today differs from the racism experienced in our nation generations ago in the form of slavery. Slavery was localized then. Racism is pervasive today. Slavery was explicit, violent, and degrading then. Racism can take many forms and functions today.

Slavery was a moral corruption commercially induced into the life of our pre-born nation. A political and religious underpinning nourished and sustained that vice over the formative years of our nation, facilitating the divide in our nation between free and slave. In that way, slavery was not considered racism but merely an acceptable social behavior by many during the Civil War era.

Similar to our divisions today, what some regard as a moral decision, others regard as a social right. For example, many believe abortion is an immoral act because it is rooted in a faith that defines life beginning at conception. Many believe it is a social decision because their faith

---

1. *And There Was Light* by Jon Meacham, p.160; Random House, 2022.

defines the beginning of life as the viability of the fetus. Some believe that abortion is legitimate during mitigating circumstances like rape, incest, or when the life of the mother is in jeopardy regardless of when life begins. In many instances, these differences exist in people of the same faith who have been divided through a deliberate manipulation of faith and politics begun many years ago.

Perhaps we can learn from Lincoln's words that "a house divided against itself cannot stand," words derived from scripture (Mark 3:24-25) embraced by people of faith on both sides of the social issues dividing our nation today. Perhaps a starting place for all in our nation, beginning with people of faith, is to realize we may all have to give up some of our liberties in order for all of us to be free. This is not an uncommon practice in our society today. We sacrifice our liberty on the highways of our nation, the airways of our skies, and the railways of our country for the sake of the safety for all.

Why there is such resistance to this same mentality over the issues of the day is perplexing but obvious. Never before has there been a deliberate politicization of faith in our country. By that, I mean a calculated decision by leaders of both a political party and the leaders of faith communities to strategize an outcome. One party of this agreement was seeking political power. The other party of this agreement was seeking denominational power by exploiting a doctrinal position.

The eventual outcome of this partnership is uncertain. But one thing is certain. A divided nation cannot stand. Scripture declares it. The history of our nation proves it. My hope and prayer are that this writing may help facilitate and further the cause of unity in our nation in some way.

PART 1

WHEN LIBERTY
ENSLAVES:
A CASE HISTORY

CHAPTER 1

An Overview
of the Times Past

One of my favorite holiday movies is *A Christmas Story*. Portraying the experiences of a young Indiana boy in the 1940s, the movie reflects many social traditions both of the season and the times. Such scenes as buying the family Christmas tree, visiting Santa at the local department store, and gathering as a family for meals in the kitchen twice daily are heartwarming reminders of a time that has passed. I find this movie endearing because it reminds me of my experiences as a child growing up in New Jersey in the 1960s. Comparing my Christmas boyhood experiences to that of an Indiana boy decades earlier, I find similar traditions being passed down through the generations.

It is only when we take the time to reflect on those times past that we get a better understanding of our present times. Our past establishes a point of reference for our present. That is why a movie like *The Christmas Story* is so effective: for many of us, it puts our past in contact with our present. In most cases, that is a good thing. Most of us enjoy the pleasures of an improved lifestyle because of the advent of new technologies over the decades. Some of us enjoy the fruits of an education our parents did not have and are able to live a different lifestyle than they did. But all of us bring forward the social traditions of our former life and are free to express them to the generations that follow us. That is the American experience of both today and of the past. However, not all the social impacts from one generation to the next have been beneficial to the well-being of our nation.

The objective of this chapter is to illustrate one such case from a time in our nation's past experiencing social phenomena similar to those in our nation today. Such a time is the mid-19th century, just prior to the Civil War. Let us begin by trying to understand the social issues of those times.

I am not a social scientist, a political analyst, or a historian. I am a person who has lived long enough to see some social traditions passed on from one generation to the next. I realize my experience is extremely limited when trying to understand generational trends in a nation. To get some clarity on how that happens, I refer to the works of current day historians. Jon Meacham, a fellow of the Society of American Historians, in one of his recent writings describes Lincoln as a politician in search of the "public sentiment" which would be a measure of perceived values and attitudes of his current society. We will use this reference for our purposes of trying to identify the social trends of his time.

AN INDICATION OF TIMES PAST

Lincoln's assessment was that the dominant social issues of his times were influenced by either one's politics, the financial implications of the issue, or the prejudice within the heart of the individual citizen. Lincoln determined that the past experience of the issue, one's faith, or appealing to one's reason did not influence the relative importance of the social issues of his times. History, faith, or reason were not compelling effects of social priorities. Politics, finances, and prejudice were.

We have the advantage of knowing Lincoln's experiences past 1859 when he was just a candidate. We know that Lincoln's presidency began on March 4, 1861, being inaugurated as the 16th president of the United

States. After his reelection four years later, he was assassinated on April 15, 1865, just 42 days into his second term. We know that what Lincoln observed in his candidacy, he realized to be true during his presidency. That is, slavery, the top social issue of his administration, was accepted in the nation because of its economic and political alignment. These were the same indications he had learned as a candidate many years earlier that influenced the social preferences in the nation. The truth was that there was a lot of money to be made in the American economy on the backs of the American slaves. It also was an issue that aligned politically with the Democratic South and which caused division in the nation after the election of a Republican president named Lincoln. Other factors had little effect on the decision to embrace slavery for many Americans in our nation at that time.

THE INTRODUCTION OF SLAVERY TO OUR NATION

Slavery, a moral corruption as viewed by us today, was commercially introduced into the life of our preborn nation. A small contingent of approximately 20 kidnapped Angolans arrived in the British colony of Virginia on August 20, 1619. At this point, the enslaved Africans were bought by the English colonists which marked the beginning of 2 1/2 centuries of slavery in America.[2] A depravity that infected our nation during its formulation took root and was present in our nation at its birth. Annette Gordon-Reed, historian, and the Carl M. Loeb University Professor at Harvard University, offers a different account of the start of slavery in our nation. The traditional historic growth in slavery is attributed to the original 20 slaves growing to four million by the time of Emancipation in 1865. Gordon–Reed contends that racially based slavery began on American soil in St. Augustine, Florida, established by the Spanish as early as 1565. Documentation of the presence of Africans in St. Augustine exists in surviving parish records and historical accounts

---

2. First enslaved Africans arrive in Jamestown, setting the stage for slavery in North America", Feb. 23, 2023; https://www.history.com/this-day-in-history/first-african-slave-ship-arrives-jamestown-colony

of the conflicts that arose between the enslaved people and their Spanish captors. In 1735, the Spanish governor chartered a settlement for enslaved Africans who escaped from the English colonies and made it to St. Augustine. The settlement of free Blacks existed until the Spanish ceded Florida to the United States in 1819.[3]

Within 60 years of the arrival of the first slaves in the colonies, slavery had become a morally, legally, and socially acceptable institution. Property owners in the southern colonies began establishing plantation farms for rice, tobacco, and sugar cane, all requiring an increasing demand for labor. Wealthy planters turned to traders who imported a vast number of slaves from West Africa. As the "inventory" increased, a new industry was born: the slave auction.[4]

These slave auctions were open markets where humans were inspected like animals, bought, and sold to the highest bidder. By the mid-19th century, a skilled and able-bodied enslaved person could be sold for up to $2,000 although prices varied by state. Slave labor became entrenched in the Southern economy. When delegates to the Constitutional Convention met in Philadelphia in the summer of 1787, approximately 700,000 enslaved people were living in the United States. The delegates were split on the moral question of slavery with its human bondage and its inhumane practices, but they were convinced of its economic necessity.[5]

Lincoln observed as a candidate for President that the growth of slavery was due to its overwhelming economic benefits to the newly formed nation. This observation was confirmed by Lincoln's experience as President. Slavery was deemed socially acceptable because it was key to the profitability of the agricultural industry of the nation. Slavery's history of human degradation made no difference. Even the degree of people's devotion to their faith made no difference. Slavery was ingrained into the social fabric of our nation.

---

3. *On Juneteenth* by Anette Gordon-Reed; P.57,61-62; Liveright Publishing Corp., 2021.

4. *How Slavery Became the Economic Engine of the South* by Gregg Timmons; March 6, 2018; www.history.com

5. *Ibid.*

SLAVERY: A LOGICAL CHOICE OF THE TIMES

It is impossible for us to relate to or identify with the circumstances under which slavery was introduced to our nation. It would be a challenge to research the attitudes of those first British colonists of Virginia, a task far beyond the scope of this writing. Yet, a quick look at the history of slavery through *The Free Encyclopedia* of Wikipedia gives us some insight.

John Locke (1632-1704) was an English philosopher and physician and was widely regarded as one of the most influential of Enlightenment thinkers and commonly known as the "father of liberalism." Locke seems to hold a distinction between legitimate and illegitimate forms of slavery. Locke, writing during the time of European expansion, argued that only the conquest of certain peoples during a just war could justify their enslavement. But Locke remained silent on the issue of African American enslavement, causing some confusion on the issue. It has been stated that John Locke's arguments regarding slavery have been cited by both abolitionist and Confederate leaders in defending their positions. In this vacuum of any clear distinction on the legitimacy of slavery in America, one can understand the acceptance of the practice purely as a business decision by the British colonists.[6]

Life in the colonies and in the early days of our nation is hard for us to imagine. The amount of labor required to run a substantial farm was not possible with only family members. Considering the lack of technology, automation, and any modern conveniences, considerable labor was required to make a living. One can imagine the difficulty in refusing to use the relatively inexpensive labor available from the slave industry. After an initial capital investment, a modest recurring expense of room and board was a relatively inexpensive solution to the labor problem. One can easily imagine compartmentalizing the use of slaves as a business decision and dismissing any thought of the morality of that decision.

---

6. *John Locke and American Slavery - Humanities at Davidson.* Downloaded from https://humes. laurenmeyers.net/john-locke-and-american-slavery, July 29, 2024.

SLAVERY: A GATEWAY TO RACISM

From our vantage point, hundreds of years after the inception of slavery in our nation, we can easily conclude that slavery is racism in its worst form. It is logical to assume that the extent of human depravity and the horror of the experience exacted on these African citizens could only be the result of racially motivated antipathy and/or indifference toward these people. However, the depths and the extent to which racism is experienced in our nation today differ substantially from the racism experienced in our nation generations ago. Racism became more complex and insidious as it has passed from generation to generation throughout our history. Originally, slavery was localized in the colonies, then spread to the southern states. Today, racism is pervasive. Slavery was explicit, violent, and degrading then. Racism can take many forms today.

In order for racism to adapt, it had to be nourished and sustained over the life of our nation. It is logical to think that the concept of slavery introduced racism to our nation. Slavery was the means used to mature racism during our nation's formative years, developing a spirit of racism by its dehumanizing tactics, leading to an abhorrence in the colonists, then throughout the southern portion of our nation, toward a people that had a darker skin pigmentation, a different language, and a different culture. This spirit of racism, initiated through slavery, passed from generation to generation, finally resulting in the form we now experience in our nation today.

The evolution of slavery was a slow, deliberate movement in the governing of our nation and in the soul of its people, requiring and acquiring political and religious underpinnings, ultimately dividing a country willing to be half slave and half free. Slavery was not considered racism by many during the Civil War era. The confluence of faith and politics during that time allowed many to support slavery while still being loyal to both their faith and their politics. Slavery was merely an acceptable social practice of the time.

The Civil War brought about the demise of slavery but not the end of racism. On the contrary, racism morphed from a socially accepted practice into the underbelly of the social structure in our nation. Gordon-Reed describes slavery as being replaced with a racial hierarchy.[7] I agree with Gordon-Reed's point. This racial hierarchy I refer to as the spirit of slavery. There, hidden from public view, racism is free to evidence itself in various forms at unpredicted times in fashion true to the spirit that it is. In this way, racism has survived being publicly scorned but privately preserved.

THE DIVIDING OF A NATION

Division of a nation as big and diverse as ours, even during its formative years, requires a physical separation of boundaries, governance, and assets—and the soul of a nation. The soul of a nation is nothing more than the composite of the individual souls in that nation acting collectively in a predetermined way.

The soul of an individual is comprised of the mind, will, and emotions. In addition, every soul is accompanied by a spirit which I characterize as an energy, an intangible source of direction that brings life to us. That is why Scripture refers to us as living beings (Genesis 2:7) with a soul (Mathew 16:26). For a nation's soul to be divided simply means the minds, wills, emotions, and spirits of the people in a nation are separating into factions.

For a nation to embrace the Civil War, more than a physical divide is required. There must be a division in the nation's collective soul to fuel the will, emotions, mind, and spirit to fight for respective causes.

A NATION PHYSICALLY DIVIDED

Civil war does not occur overnight. Barbara Walter has spent her career studying the process of civil war in many nations throughout history. Walter writes,

---

7. *On Juneteenth* by Anette Gordon-Reed; P.28; Liveright Publishing Corp., 2021.

In the Civil War, so-called Minute Men militias—who modeled themselves after the Revolutionary War-era patriots—began to crop up throughout the South as early as the 1830s, decades before the Civil War broke out. These militias were organized by small groups of radical secessionists, almost all of whom were white plantation owners, who wanted to build support for Southern independence. It took them years to rally the white working class to their cause.[8]

Declaring a physical divide of a nation requires strategies, assets and establishing a method of governance. But before any of those can be put in place, people must be recruited to the effort. This is true for any new organizational development, including a business, a political campaign, a church, or a new nation. The minute-man militia successfully achieved that purpose. Walter also notes that "it was the election of President Abraham Lincoln, the first president able to win power without the support of Southern Democrats, which convinced Southerners to secede."[9]

Walter describes how a nation can divide physically. She also states a political event such as an election is sufficient to initiate that divide. But I believe in order for a nation to successfully complete that divide it is because the soul of the nation has been divided as well.

A NATION'S SOUL DIVIDED

On Monday, March 4, 1861, Abraham Lincoln took the oath of office as President of the United States. Lincoln was elected with the majority of votes being cast for other candidates. This was due to an election determined by the electoral count being dispersed over several presidential candidates. A phenomenon we have experienced in recent presidential elections twice.

---

8. *How Civil Wars Start* by Barbara F. Walter; P.97; Random House, 2022.

9. *Ibid.*, P. 93.

The issue that divided the politics of our nation during the election of Lincoln was slavery. The issue that divided the soul of our nation was faith. This division of soul was made evident by the division in the faith communities—faith communities that shared the same faith. The mix of faith and politics had caused a new fervor and a determined resistance to unity. President Lincoln was well aware of this divide and tried to calm fears in his second inaugural speech. He addressed the fact that people reading the same Bible and praying to the same God were on both sides of the issue of slavery. Each side was invoking God's aid against the other. In his address Lincoln invoked Mathew 7:1,2 which warns Christians not to judge one another at the risk of being judged. In spite of Lincoln's comments, the opposite took place. The South felt judged by the North for their moral superiority. The North felt judged by the South for their preference to preserve the union over slavery.

In the hours just before dawn on April 12, 1861, in Charleston Harbor, South Carolina the first shots were fired on Fort Sumter from Confederate batteries. "The last ray of hope for preserving the Union peaceably expired at the assault upon Fort Sumter," Lincoln remarked. On Saturday, April 13 Lincoln made his intentions clear by writing "And, in every event, I shall to the extent of my ability, repel force by force."[10] Our nation was at war.

FAITH ADAPTING TO POLITICAL PREFERENCES

When people of faith embrace a social outcome that hurts other people, it results in a spiritual consequence. That is, a conscious decision to embrace a practice that violates the fundamentals of one's faith changes the perspective of one's faith. To embrace slavery with its complement of violent behaviors and dehumanizing tendencies is a clear violation of some of the basic tenets of the Christian faith. Even those scriptures that refer to the servant/master relationship allude to God's watchful eye for the sincerity of heart and concern for one another in that relationship

---

10. *Ibid.,* P.237-238.

(Ephesians 6:1-6). The ability to ignore or interpret scripture in such a way as to accommodate different political interpretations is referred to in scripture as "a spirit of stupor" (Romans 11:8). For the purposes of this writing, I describe this phenomenon as a "spirit of racism" being passed from generation to generation. It is a spiritual dynamic that affects people's faith and allows them to accommodate their political preferences.

This issue will be discussed in detail in the next two chapters. However, let's illustrate from the days of Lincoln examples of how views of faith can change over time with the changing of a nation's political landscape.

It has been well documented that influential Christian ministers of various denominations were hypocritical in their approach to slavery. Many would initially describe slavery as "evil" only to reverse their position years later to describe it as divinely sanctioned and should be defended out of duty to God.

Slavery Ordained of God published in 1850s by a Presbyterian minister stated that if a pro-slavery Christian decided that God willed a particular slave to continue as a slave, he would thereby retain his own position as a slave. If that pro-slavery Christian decided that God willed a slave to be free, the slave thereby had the right to be free. This view was a widely accepted Christian view in the middle of the 19th century.

Knowing "God's will" has been a subject debated over the centuries for all communities of faith. My personal belief is that regardless of our best efforts we are not able to fully comprehend the mind and heart of God. However, in trying to determine if our actions are according to God's plans as a bare minimum they should not be in conflict with scripture. As mentioned previously, the tendency is to ignore or interpret scripture in such a way as to accommodate different political interpretations. The lesson to be learned through this example is the heart of this writing. That is, the confluence of faith and politics is a toxic blending of soul and spirit that only divides communities of faith. In this case, embracing "the Ross argument" assigns God's will to a fickleness that randomly grants freedom or bondage for a subject based on a third-party appeal. That sounds more like a lottery than a sovereign God Creator of all mankind. That is the result of the confluence of faith and politics.

People of the same Christian faith developed different perspectives of their faith to support their political position with regard to slavery. Or was it the other way around? Did their political position affect their faith? I think we see a little of both in the days of Lincoln, and I believe it to be true currently in our experience today. Sometimes, one's faith shapes one's politics. Sometimes, one's politics cause one to rethink the perspectives of faith. I know this to be true in my own experience of faith and politics.

THE PRICE OF ENSLAVEMENT

There is a price paid by all in a nation for the enslavement of some. It does not matter whether it is a literal enslavement of one's life or the enslavement of liberty once held. Both the enslaved and the free share the consequences of the times. President Lincoln's words and reflections on his views of slavery are well recorded in our history. He used words like hate when describing his feelings concerning the subject. He described slavery as a monstrous injustice. He also understood that embracing slavery reflected badly on how other countries viewed our nation. Outside free institutions would view us as hypocrites and doubt our sincerity with regard to freedom while criticizing our Declaration of Independence.

President Lincoln knew that if only part of a nation supported enslavement, the reputation of the entire nation would be diminished. All people of all nations that respect liberty would judge the actions of some in our country to represent our entire nation as a whole. In other words, all of us are painted with the same brush of embracing the enslavement of others regardless of our position on the issue. It was true in the days of Lincoln, and it is true today. If we as a nation tolerate the enslavement of some, we are embracing the concept of slavery for all. History has shown it is a short step between those two extremes.

I would like to close this chapter with a recent illustration of just how close these two extremes exist to one another in our nation today.

At the time of this writing, South Carolina is considering proposed legislation that treats abortion as murder and applies penalties accordingly. The South Carolina Prenatal Equal Protection Act (H.3549) would "afford equal protection of the laws to all preborn children from the moment of fertilization" and reclassify any act that ends a pregnancy as "willful prenatal homicide." This means that an abortion could be punished like any murder, with sentences at a minimum of years in prison to, conceivably, the death penalty, though the latter isn't spelled out in the bill. There are no exceptions for rape or incest, though the bill does allow one if a woman "was compelled to do so by the threat of imminent death or great bodily injury."

U.S. Representative Nancy Mace (R-S.C) is a pro-life Republican, whose testimony is that she was raped at 16, is "deeply passionate" about this issue. She is quoted as saying "It's unbelievable to me that this is where we are. My [pro-life] record is almost 100 percent, but this is an American issue. Execute a woman for abortion? It's also hypocritical. You can't be pro-life and then kill a woman for having an abortion."[11]

Clearly, we have lost our way when our legislators are confused by the proposed legislation that they are sponsoring. This is an example that Lincoln's thoughts are valid for today. When some people in our nation are enslaved, we are all guilty of embracing slavery in some form, regardless of our positions. Rep. Mace has confirmed that for us.

---

11. "South Carolina's Iran-like crackdown on women" by Kathleen Parker, *Washington Post*, March 19, 2023.

CHAPTER 2

The Land of the Free

In September 1814, our nation's war with the United Kingdom, known as the War of 1812, was in its third year. The British had sacked the capitol city of Washington and torched the White House while taking prisoners. Among the prisoners was a popular doctor from Prince George's County in Maryland. A friend of the doctor, a 35-year-old lawyer named Francis Scott Key, sailed on a ship flying a truce flag to negotiate a prisoner exchange with the Royal Navy.

The mission was successful, with the British commanders agreeing to free the doctor, but the doctor and his friend would not be allowed to leave the vessel until a surprise attack on Baltimore had been completed. That's how Key ended up witnessing the bombardment of Fort McHenry while aboard a British ship. As he witnessed the battle, from his vantage point he could not tell who had won or lost.

At dawn, Key saw the American flag, 15 stars and 15 stripes at the time, still waving over the fort and was inspired to write a poem. Soon, it was set to the same tune that exists today and came to be known as "The Star-Spangled Banner."[12]

AN ANTHEM OF FREEDOM

The "Star-Spangled Banner" was first recognized for official use by the U.S. Navy in 1889. On March 3, 1931, President Herbert Hoover signed into law a joint resolution passed by the U.S. Congress making the song the official national anthem of the United States.[13] It is a song we all have been accustomed to hearing played at most sporting events in our nation, professional and amateur competitions alike. All of us are usually stirred when we hear this song played during Olympic competitions with athletes from our country standing on the award platforms with medals draped over their shoulders. At those moments, there is no doubt in our minds that we are a blessed nation because we are "the home of the brave" and "the land of the free" as the song dramatically states in its conclusion.

Or are we? Maybe we have not been such a land of freedom for all, all the time. Maybe we have not been so brave to face that part of our history. The version of the "Star-Spangled Banner" we sing today is not the form of the original verse. The writing was originally called "The Defense of Fort M'Henry." The second half of the third verse ends like this:

> *No refuge could save the hireling and slave*
> *From the terror of flight or gloom of the grave,*
> *And the star-spangled banner in triumph doth wave*
> *O'er the land of the free and the home of the brave.*

THOSE EXEMPTED FROM FREEDOM

It was the British practice to force the conscription of American sailors to fight for the Royal Navy. In addition, the British promised refuge to

---

12. "The ugly reason 'The Star-Spangled Banner' didn't become our national anthem for a century" by Gillian Brockwell, *The Washington Post*, October 18, 2020.

13. Wikipedia, The Free Encyclopedia, The Star-Spangled Banner; 36 U.S. Code 301- National anthem

any enslaved black people who escaped their enslavers. Men who escaped their bonds of slavery were welcome to join the British Corps of Colonial Marines in exchange for land after their service. An estimated 4,000 people escaped from Virginia and Maryland through the Royal Navy. The original text written by Key refers to the recruitment and hiring of the slaves, along with the implied revenge by the American victory that night.

These lyrics clearly reference the Colonial Marines, according to Jefferson Morley, author of *Snowstorm in August: Washington City, Francis Scott Key, and the Forgotten Race Riot of 1835*. They are meant to scorn and threaten the former African American slaves who took the British up on their offer. Key surely knew about the Colonial Marines, and it's even possible he saw them among the contingent of British ships that sailed into Baltimore Harbor.[14]

AN ANTHEM WITH A CONTEXT

I have sung the National Anthem an untold number of times during my lifetime, as have most of us. In all those times, never has the thought of slavery come to my mind. I am not sure that black people in our nation feel the same. Obviously, Colin Kaepernick felt differently.

Colin Rand Kaepernick is an American civil rights activist and a football quarterback who is now a free agent. He played six seasons for the San Francisco 49ers in the National Football League. In 2016, he knelt during the national anthem at the start of NFL games in protest of police brutality and racial inequality in the United States. He has not played in the NFL since.[15]

Kaepernick's actions were not received kindly by the NFL owners and was even the target of criticism from the president at the time, Donald J. Trump. What resulted was a protracted discussion concerning players' rights and the power of the owner's prerogatives concerning players'

---

14. "The ugly reason 'The Star-Spangled Banner' didn't become our national anthem for a century" by Gillian Brockwell, The Washington Post, October 18, 2020.

15. Wikipedia, The Free Encyclopedia, *USA Today*, Nov. 16, 2019.

social views. While slavery was never mentioned during this experience to my knowledge, one can make a connection between the racism being experienced today to the slavery that existed in our country many years ago. I would describe that connection to be a similar spirit between the slave owners of the past and those guilty of racist actions today. Both have the same target for their actions: people of any skin color that is not white. Both have the same motive: to restrict the liberties of the targeted people. One is clear as we examine the history of our nation. The other is evident in our current national experience.

But how have these racist subtleties in our nation's history, like the original language of our national anthem, evaded exposure? Why were the traces of racism excluded from the discussion of our nation's past in some fashion when we were first taught in our primary and secondary public schools? At least they were many years ago when I experienced my education directly and my children's education indirectly. Let's examine another's childhood educational experience in the state of Texas.

A HISTORY REVEALED IN PART

Historian Annette Gordon-Reed remembers Texas state history being taught in both her fourth and seventh grade education experiences without slavery being mentioned. If it was mentioned it was characterized with regard to states' rights whether to embrace it or not. In her case any educational void regarding slavery was satisfied by the experiences of her parents and grandparents. Gordon-Reed's point is that the history she was taught was emphasized as a state's right to pursue statehood. Slavery was not the key issue with regard to the Civil War. The slow adoption of the truth about slavery in her home state is described in her writing *On Juneteenth*.

June 19, 1865, was the day that enslaved African Americans in Texas were told that slavery had ended, two years after the Emancipation Proclamation had been signed, and just over two months after Confederate General Robert E. Lee had surrendered to Ulysses S. Grant at Appomattox. Despite the formal surrender, the Confederate army continued to fight on in Texas until mid-May. It was only after they finally surrendered that Major General Gordon Granger, while at his headquarters in Galveston, prepared General Order Number 3, announcing the end of legalized slavery in the state.

It took two years for news of the Emancipation Proclamation to reach the borders of Texas. Granted there was no internet, Facebook, or Twitter to advance news as it does today. Even considering the slow pace of mail in those days, limited telegraphing, and limited access to such a remote part of the nation, it does seem amazing that no indication of such a monumental decision affecting a large portion of our nation's population at the time was so slow in arriving. By contrast, it took only a few months for word concerning Lee's surrender to reach Texas. One can surmise that the news curtailing the war to preserve slavery was more important than the news that curtailed slavery in Texas. The first curtailed the loss of white people's lives. The second curtailed the loss of black people's lives.

While Gordon-Reed's specific perspective is the effect of slavery on the formulation of the state of Texas, similar experiences occurred throughout our nation. Before the Civil War, the fight for slavery's acceptance was raging over the many territories that were now seeking to be included in the Union. The issue was either to include slavery in the expansion of the United States or keep it confined to the Southern states to die a slow death by attrition. At stake was the issue as to whether our nation would truly remain "the Land for the Free" or would settle into a nation of being a free land for only some of the people.

These aspects regarding the Civil War and the expansion of our nation were not included in U.S. History classes when Gordon-Reed attended school as a child in Texas nor for me as a child being educated in a different state as part of a different generation. Not having been in a U.S. history class recently in our nation's schools, I assume that the social/political underpinnings associated with slavery still are not discussed throughout our nation today. When these issues are included in some fashion of contemporary schools, they usually make the headlines of the national media expressing the resistance to such a curriculum. The absence of this discourse in the classroom results in a lack of understanding as to how an evil like slavery persisted for so many years. Perhaps if we knew the answer to that question, it would help us confront the racism that permeates our nation today.

In my educational experience, the history of our nation described slavery as the principal cause of the division in our country that led to the Civil War. Although different from Gordon-Reed's experience, my experience was similar in that slavery was presented casually, including some specifics like the Dred Scott decision and the 13th amendment to the Constitution, both to be discussed at length in a later chapter. In presenting slavery this way, we divorce the social linkages embedded in the spirit of our nation of the slavery of times past from those linkages to the racism of times present. The result is we permit the false impression that we have been and still are "a land of the free" for all in our nation at all times.

ACQUIRING LAND FOR SLAVERY'S EXPANSION

Slavery could not have spread beyond the Southern states without political influence. Political leaders often are divided over social issues. What results is a conspiracy of efforts on the local, national, and international levels to achieve a desired political outcome. That is true today and was true back in the 18th century.

The Missouri Territory was part of the 800,000 square miles bought from France in the Louisiana Purchase of 1803. In 1818, the nation was deeply divided into pro- and anti-slavery factions when the Missouri Territory first applied for statehood. It was clear that many in the territory wanted to allow slavery in the new state. If approved, Missouri would have been the first state west of the Mississippi River to allow slavery within its borders.

The Missouri Compromise of 1820 admitted Missouri to the Union as a state that allowed slavery and Maine as a free state. It was a political compromise preserving the delicate balance between slave and free states. It also banned slavery from the remaining Louisiana purchase lands and remained in force for over 30 years. This legislation managed to temporarily keep the peace, but it failed to resolve the long-term question of slavery in our nation. Southerners opposed the compromise because it set a precedent for Congress to make laws concerning slavery. Northerners disliked the law because it meant slavery was expanding into the new territory.[16]

Slavery was spreading to other areas of our nation as well. Stephen F. Austin was described as a Virginia-born, Missouri-raised moving to Texas while it was still a Mexican province. Austin had come to Texas not to create cattle ranches but to produce profitable cotton fields. The Mexican government was eager to have Americans come and develop the Texas area; however, there was a strong anti-slavery sentiment in the country. Austin and his Tejano (ethnic Mexicans living in Texas) partners convinced Mexican legislators to protect slavery as a way of ensuring the success of their colonization effort. When Texans successfully rebelled against Mexico and set up the Republic of Texas in 1836 the issue was settled. With this move, the right to enslave was secured, and the White settlers poured into the new republic.[17] The future of Texas being admitted into the Union was resolved with the election of Polk as President of the United States.

POLK'S ADVANCE OF SLAVERY

James Knox Polk was elected the 11th president of the United States, serving from 1845 to 1849. Polk won a close election with 49.5% of the popular vote. Polk's victory was his advocacy of the annexation of Texas. Henry Clay, his opponent, was opposed to it.

It was well known in the political circles of the times that Mexico threatened war if the United States annexed Texas. Armed conflict and a declaration of war came after a controversial April 1846 skirmish between U.S. and Mexican troops in territory along the Rio Grande. By late 1847, U.S. Forces had prevailed, and Polk arranged for a $15 million

---

16. https://www.history.com/topics/slavery/missouri-compromise; History.com, June 27, 2023.
17. *On Juneteenth by* Annette Gordon-Reed; P. 24; Liveright Publishing Company, 2021.

purchase price for the territory that became known as the Mexican Cession. Mexican-owned land would eventually come to comprise all or parts of Arizona, California, Colorado, Kansas, Nevada, New Mexico, Oklahoma, Utah, and Wyoming.

As our nation expanded, it remained deeply divided over the issue of slavery. A nation divided over social issues will produce a nation that is politically divided. This is as today as it was during the days of slavery. Social division creates a politically charged environment in the governance of our country.

SLAVERY AND THE CONSTITUTION

All governance in our nation is bound by and finds its authority through the Constitution of the United States. But the intent of the Constitution may be interpreted in many ways. This was especially the case with regard to slavery. Also, legislation written earlier in our nation's experience (to be discussed next) caused additional conflict among the lawmakers. In spite of what our Declaration of Independence states, not all lawmakers of that time believed that all men were created equally.

The Northwest Ordinance of 1787, the earliest legislation to have an impact on lawmakers, proposed a legal structure for the settlement of land in five present-day states: Ohio, Indiana, Illinois, Michigan, and Wisconsin. Ratified by Congress on July 13, 1787, the Northwest Ordinance prohibited enslavement in territories north of the Ohio River—the first federal law to address slavery. In addition, the Northwest Ordinance created a 3-step process for new territories to become states.[18]

Regardless of this precedent-setting early legislation, the interpretation of the Constitution itself marked the greatest disagreement among lawmakers. Article 1 Section 2 of the Constitution directs states to count the number of free persons, add to it the number enslaved multiplied by 3/5, and subtract the number of Indians within that state to determine the

---

18. *"Northwest Ordinance of 1787."* by Robert McNamara ThoughtCo, Feb. 17, 2021, downloaded from https:thoughtco.com/northwest-ordinance-of-1787-4177006.

number of people in a state to be represented and taxed. These conditions were eliminated by the passing and ratification of the Fourteenth Amendment Section Two on July 9, 1868.

However, even Lincoln was conflicted over his long-held position that the government had no power to abolish slavery where it existed. Lincoln's position was that the Founders fully embraced the concept of "all men created equal" but recognized it would take some time for that concept to be embraced with regard to the enslaved of our nation. They recognized that slavery was embedded in the nature of our nation from the beginning, and they were willing to let the country have the time to mature and correct this fundamental flaw of liberty.

A HISTORY DESTINED TO BE REPEATED

We have all heard something like the expression "Those who don't know history are destined to repeat it." Wikipedia tells us various such statements can be attributed to either Edmund Burke, an Anglo-Irish politician, or George Santayana, a Spanish philosopher, poet, and novelist. Both men are of considerable distinction and worthy of being known for more than an expression they may or may not have made. However, it seems to be appropriate to reference a phrase like this at this point in this writing.

The social and political circumstances that collided many years ago in the history of our nation to bring about the Civil War seem to be reappearing in a similar form in our nation today. While the concern is not over a renewed outbreak of slavery, we are witness to a similar curtailing of liberties. Our present-day experience does not require the addition of more land to expand the violation of liberties to additional people. It requires the tampering of the political electoral boundaries of each state to restrict people's liberties. Today's threats to our liberties do not require baiting a neighboring country into war to expand our sphere of influence in exploiting the liberties of people. All it takes is our elected officials tampering with our nation's internal controls over justice and liberty through the three (Executive, Legislative and Judicial) branches of our government. The effect is not a redistribution of property, but rather a redistribution of liberty throughout our nation. Just as in the days of Lincoln when states were labeled as pro and anti-slavery, we now can label our nation in terms of blue states and red states, pro-life and pro-choice states and pro-gun and anti-gun law states.

Just as we can sense a tangible divide in our nation over social issues, the effects of slavery are still felt by many in our nation due to racism. I offer the following results of a recent poll as an illustration of the residual impact of slavery still being felt today in our nation through racism.

A Post-Ipsos (Washington Post and Ipsos is a global market research and public opinion company) poll found "Sixty-nine percent of Black Americans say it is a 'more dangerous' time today to be a Black teenager than when they were teenagers. Just four percent say it is a less dangerous time while 25% describe the environment for teenagers as being 'about the same'. Nearly six in 10 Black adults say they are very or somewhat worried that they or someone they love will be attacked because they are Black."[19]

This same poll indicates that "concerns about public stances in certain states extend to Black Americans' belief that they are not getting a fair shake from the country's political system. Nearly eight in 10 Black Americans also say they have 'very little' or just 'some' political power in the United States." [20]

A recent example of these racist trends in politics was also cited in this poll. "Over 6 in 10 Black adults say they were worried when GOP lawmakers in the Tennessee House voted this spring to expel state representatives Justin Jones and Justin Pearson, both Black Democrats, for leading a gun-control rally at the Capitol. They were reinstated to the body after votes by local officials."[21]

I realize this is one poll, but it is safe to say it offers anecdotal evidence of similar fears to those of the enslaved people in our nation many years

19. "Poll: Black Americans more upbeat but fear worsening racism" by Tim Craig, Emily Guskin, and Scott Clement; *Washington Post*, Sunday, June 18, 2023.
20. *Ibid.*
21. *Ibid.*

ago. My alarm is rooted in the many other instances of violence toward black people that we read about in our nation's daily news. My deep concern is based on my faith experience in Evangelical communities over many years. I believe our nation is facing a crisis in our collective faith experience.

A CRISIS OF FAITH THEN AND NOW

Scripture describes that *liberty vs. enslavement* is fundamental to our faith.

- Our faith expresses our *liberty* from a previous life when we were *enslaved* to destructive behaviors. (Galatians 5:1)

- Our faith connects us to God in a fashion that creates *liberty* in all our relationships to love one another and not be *enslaved* by bitter envy and jealousy. (2 Corinthians 3:17)

- Our faith gives us an understanding of boundaries that provide *liberty* to live life to its fullest and not be *enslaved* by destructive habits. (John 8:32)

- Our faith *liberates* us to serve others and not be *enslaved* by our desires. (Galatians 5:13)

Understanding the significance of the relationship between *liberty* and *enslavement* in our faith experience is fundamental to living a faith that is relevant to both our past and our present. This understanding connects us to the history of our nation so that we can better identify with the torment of a people constrained to live without the freedoms afforded so many others in the nation. This understanding connects us to the present in an ability to relate to people of the same faith who do not have the same perspectives on the social issues of the day. Once we can see social issues from a perspective different from ours, our faith frees us from judging others for having a different perspective. Our faith enables us to see other perspectives not as being wrong, but as being different. Recognizing a faith different from my own neither invalidates my faith nor does it validate the other. It simply means we see things differently. Let's leave the judging up to God, who is better equipped for the job.

This understanding of the relationship between *liberty vs enslavement* is critical to the political posturing that embraces our country today. As a people of faith, we must realize we are not going to convince anyone that our faith position on social issues is correct by attacking them and restricting their liberties. Taking one's liberty away is requiring them to comply with a conviction that they do not have. This forced compliance will do nothing to convince them otherwise. It will only enhance the desire to live free as they once did before their liberty was taken away.

The solution to our problem of the day will not be attained by annexing the political territories of our nation and binding them to a rule of law that is perceived as enslavement. All that does is create civil unrest which will eventually lead to anarchy and civil war. Our history speaks of that experience. The experts who study civil war throughout history agree.

Most Americans cannot imagine another civil war in their country. They assume our democracy is too resilient, too robust to devolve into conflict. Or they assume that our country is too wealthy and advanced to turn on itself. Or they assume that any rebellion would quickly be stamped out by our powerful government, giving the rebels no chance. They see the Whitmer kidnapping plot, or even the storming of the U.S. Capitol, as isolated incidents, the frustrated acts of a small group of violent extremists. But this is because they don't know how civil wars start.[22]

---

22. *How Civil Wars Start* by Barbara F. Walter; P. xviii, Crown; 2022.

CHAPTER 3

Liberty for All

I grew up living in a predominately white, modest New Jersey community as part of a second-generation Italian family. Looking back, it is easy to understand why the plight of Black Americans in our nation at that time was not emphasized. Now, I realize my family was still emerging from its own plight at the time.

My grandfather immigrated to this country with his parents and siblings and with little to no education or skills. My father made his way with less than an eighth-grade education. They worked hard and served our country during times of war, my grandfather during World War I and my father and his brothers during World War II. They never talked about their own plights. So, it makes sense that they would not talk about the plights of others.

That family background, combined with being bussed one hour each way to a private, predominately white, Catholic school in North Jersey, sealed my social isolation from any exposure to racial confrontation. The closest thing to that experience was in the sixth grade when there was an influx of Cuban refugee girls into the school. Several dark-skinned students were immersed in classes with little knowledge of the English language. Consequently, the immigrant girls stayed mainly to themselves, and social interaction was severely limited. They were quiet and polite and offered no information about their flight from Cuba. We never thought to ask. We had more important matters during recess, like baseball and touch football.

One tradition that stands out in my memory from those formative years in grade school is that every morning we would be unloaded from our respective buses and ushered into the auditorium. It was odd for the room to be referred to as the "auditorium" because it had no permanent seating. It did have a large, curtained stage at the end opposite the descending stairs of the entrance and a highly polished marble-like floor. Most days it was without the folding chairs that were put up for assemblies and concerts. Here every morning the student body would assemble to hear morning announcements and pledge our allegiance to the flag. Informing the student body of the ongoing racial tensions in our nation at that time was not a high priority in my grade school experience, but the liberty afforded to us by living in our nation was emphasized every day through the reciting of that pledge. That act drove into the subconscious mind of each child that we lived in a country that was established for both liberty and justice even though we were unable to fully comprehend the meaning of it all.

THE CONTEXT OF THE PLEDGE

Most of us have been raised reciting the Pledge of Allegiance on innumerable occasions. In so doing, we are offering a sign of our faithfulness not to an ornamental piece of starred and striped material called a flag but to the form of government that is represented by the flag. In our case, it is a republic, which means it is headed by a Chief of State, which is our president, not a monarch.

Our pledge is made not to just any type of a republic. We are pledging our loyalty to a republic that is united, not capable of being divided, and which provides *all* of its inhabitants with both liberty and justice. We fully understand that liberty cannot be allowed without constraint. If liberty in our nation were unconstrained, we could drive as fast as we wanted, anytime we wanted. We also could drive intoxicated if we wanted to do so. We willingly restrict our liberty of driving for the greater good of the nation. That is liberty with justice.

WHEN LIBERTY AND JUSTICE CONFLICT

The concepts of liberty and justice are not always as clearly defined as driving an automobile. Sometimes, one's view of justice becomes blurred or changes when political beliefs conflict with other values of individual experience. Faith, education, environmental, and economic factors influence our views of justice and liberty. Often, the view of one or the other must be adjusted to conform to our life experiences. If we adjust our perspective of justice, then our view of liberty may change as well.

An example of this changing perspective of justice and liberty is currently being experienced in our nation. Within the last few months, my home state of Maryland and the neighboring state of Virginia both approved marijuana's legal commercial sale. This was a gradual change in both liberty and justice which has occurred throughout our nation regarding the sale of this commodity.

This type of give-and-take adjustment occurs throughout our lives. Often, the result is that people who share the same faith, educational level, or many common experiences can be on opposite sides of a political or social issue despite their commonalities.

OUR VIEWS OF LIBERTY SHAPED AT AN EARLY AGE

Much of who we are and what we believe to be important for the shaping of our lives is rooted in how we were raised during our early formative years. It is true today for you and me. It is true today for our children and our children's children. It was true in the days of Lincoln as well.

Lincoln came from a family of Puritans, a religious denomination that did not support slavery on moral grounds. Later, he belonged to several Baptist churches in the areas where he lived—South Fork Baptist and Little Mount Separate Baptist churches in Kentucky and Little Pigeon Creek Baptist Church in Indiana—where opposition to slavery was a common theme.

Thus, Abraham Lincoln grew up, surrounded by antislavery preaching. Like all of us, his views evolved. While he never declared himself a believer and did not join his family's church, he did ultimately accept the moral case against slavery.

In my case, the faith I experienced as a child, a youth, and a young adult is similar to the faith experience I have today, differing only in beliefs and customs. Alternatively, the faith experience I provided for my daughter in her formative years is not similar to the faith experience she has today. There is nothing unusual about that, but the purpose here is to bring clarity in terms of this case study and its application to our experience today by pointing out that President Lincoln's experiences shaped his views on liberty and justice in a process similar to the way your experience and mine today shape our views on these same issues: shaped over time, with experience, and then applied to the context of our daily living.

At this point, I would like to focus on the effect faith had on shaping the views of liberty in the times of the Civil War. In so doing, I think we will see an eerie similarity to our times today and our views on social issues.

BLENDING OF FAITH, POLITICS, AND SOCIAL ISSUES

The mixing of faith and politics during the Civil War era has proven to be both uncomplicated and convoluted. Uncomplicated because the various positions of faith communities with regard to slavery are well documented. Convoluted because this mixture is filled with contradictions to the basic principles of the Christian faith being employed.

The practice of accepting slavery contradicts a core principle of the Christian faith. The prophet Isaiah talks about feeding the hungry, housing the poor, and clothing the naked so that "healing shall spring forth" and that "righteousness shall go before you" (Isaiah 58:8). In other words, take care of the physical aspect of people's welfare first so that they would be open to the faith message. Even Jesus saw the importance of food and other necessities of life during His ministry, prompting the miracle of feeding thousands with a few fish and loaves of bread. (Mathew 14:19). To preach the necessity of faith to Black Americans with total disregard for their physical plight is contrary to the very heart of God's message of grace and mercy.

Unlike the First Great Awakening (1730s to 1770s) in the Christian Church, a period of increased church attendance and devotion to scripture and God, which did not address slavery but focused on such ideas as predestination and the grace of God, the Second Great Awakening (approx.1800-1830+) played into this convoluted blending of faith and politics with a focus on slavery. Religious faith became a core of the debates over slavery and freedom. Both abolitionists and advocates presented biblical arguments in support of their positions.

Biblical references for proslavery theology included the curse of Ham as related in the Book of Genesis. (Genesis 9:18*ff*). Further, Abraham's having slaves was taken as a sanction for the practice. The Book of Leviticus was often quoted with its references to bondmen and bondmaids. Likewise, the Book of Exodus provides some instructions in managing slaves. The New Testament quotations from the epistles counseling slaves and servants to obey their masters are cited along with Paul's letter returning a runaway slave to his master. Perhaps most important was Jesus' lack of expressed disapproval on the subject. Neither did he express approval while simply acknowledging the existence of servants and masters in Jewish society of the time through instructions such as slaves not being above the master and the need for slaves to be hardworking (Matthew 10:24; Matthew 24:45-46). It is important to note that the type of slavery during biblical times was not the same as slavery in our nation during Lincoln's days. Biblical slavery was a form of indentured service structured around a work agreement usually to settle a debt. The slavery in our nation in the 1800s was chattel slavery that used people for labor, sex, and breeding while being exchanged like a commodity for money, guns, and/or animals. For our discussion, any references to slavery are referring to the latter, chattel slavery.

So, we had people in the same community of faith, using the same Biblical authority but arriving at opposite sides of the same issue of slavery. Some bible-believing Christians were pro-slavery while some bible-believing Christians were anti-slavery.

This practice of applying biblical experiences to current circumstances is as typical today as it was during the 1800s. Biblical accounts are given for purposes of instruction and guidance in the faith, but they always must be considered in the context of the times and the biblical principle being illustrated. The passages referred to earlier are instructions of order, respect for authority, and humility to believers. This makes sense when the context relates to the role of an indentured servant. These servants were to work off their debt in humility to their authority. These verses were never meant to be a tacit approval of chattel slavery which treated human life with degradation and contempt. This type of behavior conflicts with many other biblical principles that guide biblical faith as mentioned previously.

This example of conflicting interpretations of scripture within the same faith community was as true in the days of Lincoln as it is today. Most of the divisions in faith communities today are not over differences as stark as those between types of slavery. Most divisions today are over doctrinal differences. For example, the difference between Pentecostal and non-Pentecostal faith communities are differences in the applicability of scriptural references for the current times. The existence of differences in scriptural applications for different faith communities does not make either faith experience invalid or one faith experience more meaningful than the other. Unfortunately, these doctrinal differences are exploited through politicization which causes the amplification of these differences. Often political terms like *liberal* or *conservative* work into our descriptions of various faith communities.

The tenets of our faith will affect our views of social issues. Politics indirectly mixes with faith by endorsing a social position. By advocating a strong position on a social issue, a particular political party will appeal to a portion of a faith community with that same position on that social issue.

For example, in the politics of today, one political party has pro-life advocacy in its party platform and is generally described as being conservative. The other has pro-choice advocacy and is generally described as being liberal. Members of the same faith community are on both sides of this issue, some being pro-life, others being pro-choice. One Christian will be assumed to be conservative based on his or her political choice, the other as liberal based on his or her political choice. These labels are arbitrary and capricious because they usually relate to a person's views on social issues that are physically, socially, and spiritually complex. This is the reason that politics mixed with faith is toxic and divisive. It minimizes social discourse over complex issues and aligns the faith community into political camps that encourage division in our nation. This happened in the days of Lincoln, and it is happening today. The political names and players may change, but the methods remain the same.

A NEW CONCEPT INTRODUCED

I detailed in Chapter One how the early colonists of our country looked to the philosophies and writings of their parent country to guide their acceptance of slavery. What was emphasized in that reference were the economic benefits of slavery as a cheap source of labor for an agrarian society. This is only one dimension of the acceptance of slavery in our nation, but it is a critical element of the experience of those times. Economic pressures will cause anyone to listen to alternatives that will help alleviate the economic stresses of life. The need for cheap labor would have created a receptive audience for new thinking with regard to justice, freedom, and/or faith in our nation at that time. It is logical to think people would have been open to new concepts in any or all of these three areas if it meant easing their burden of survival.

Any change in values like freedom, justice, or faith take time to transition, particularly so in the case of faith because faith involves beliefs based on centuries of interpretation and application of core principles. The transition in views of faith evident during Lincoln's time occurred gradually. Approximately 50-75 years elapsed between the First and Second Great Awakening in the history of the Christian Church. It generally requires time to change the minds and hearts of a faith community. That was the case concerning slavery.

The history of slavery spans many cultures, nationalities, and religions from ancient times to the present day. Both Christians and Muslims captured and enslaved each other during centuries of warfare in the Mediterranean and Europe. Even Christians were given the understanding that it was acceptable to enslave people of other faiths. There was no judgment made in terms of the inferiority of the subjugated people. It was assumed that this was the plight of a conquered people and as a result were treated inhumanly. But Christianity changed its view of slavery during the early development of the Western world.

Now there were arguments in place to embrace a new concept in our nation, one that permitted us as a nation to still offer liberty and justice, just not for all. It required only an adjustment to our definitions of liberty and justice and, in some cases, an adjustment to our faith.

These three pillars of liberty, justice, and faith are foundational to the support of our nation. Instability in one or more of these areas results in freedom for some, but not all.

LIBERTY FOR SOME DIVIDES RELATIONSHIP

The nation quickly followed the path to division, the natural fruit of a dysfunctional relationship. Schisms appeared in Protestant denominations, and in 1844 the Methodist church divided into sectional churches after a dispute over the ownership of slaves by Georgia's Bishop James Andrew. The following year, the Baptists followed suit, forming a Southern Baptist Convention, which was proslavery. Then came the Presbyterians. The compelling question was: If the church could not resolve the slavery question without internal fighting, would the country be able to do so without external fighting (i.e. civil war)?

There are very few relationships, none that I am aware of, that can last without the equal foundation of liberty, justice, and faith. We must live in any relationship freely, fairly, and with faith. I recommend a faith based on a belief in God, but if that is not acceptable to the parties in the relationship it must be at least with faith in each other. Accepting anything less will result in division, conflict, and eventual destruction of the relationship. I know this from my personal experience as a husband, a father, a pastor, a counselor, and a friend. We all know this to be true, but we seem destined to repeat this dysfunction in our individual lives and presently in the life of our nation.

AN IMPERFECT UNION

The founding fathers of our nation were truly a group of inspired individuals to visualize a construct of government that would deliver universal liberty and justice. They gave us a constitution that delivered a framework to achieve this purpose. In fact, liberty and justice have been experienced by most within our nation for many years. Our founding fathers knew our nation would never achieve perfection. They said so in their preamble to the Constitution. "We the People of the United States, *in Order to form a more perfect Union, establish Justice …. And secure the Blessings of Liberty …."*

They knew it would take an evolution, a maturing in the nation, and a movement toward perfection to achieve these goals of liberty and justice for all. They were aware of the insidious threat of slavery but believed we would work through it and all the other impediments that would confront us while trying to achieve those goals. They envisioned a nation that might never achieve perfection but would constantly strive to attain it.

Our nation was derailed from the path to "a more perfect union" when the faith communities became divided over the issue of slavery.

LIBERTY AND FAITH

I can remember sitting in what I believe was a fifth-grade classroom and listening to the teacher recount the story of Patrick Henry. I don't remember the particulars about Mr. Henry other than his speech at the time was a critical influence in turning the tide of the Revolutionary War in our nation's history. I remember the words "Give me liberty or give me death" stirred in my own heart the question whether I have the audacity to make such a claim. Of course, I knew I would not for I had not developed an understanding of the power of the word *liberty* at such an early age. I knew liberty meant to be free, but at that time I equated freedom to not having any homework that evening and having the liberty to watch my favorite TV program. It is not until we live long enough and experience bondage that we can truly understand liberty. Bondage comes in many forms. It may be physical, psychological, and/or emotional. Liberty also comes in different forms and different contexts.

Physical liberty is the freedom to do as one pleases and the freedom from physical restraint. We willingly constrain our physical liberty for the benefit of the general welfare and the greater good of our nation. We willingly sacrifice some of our personal physical liberty to live in harmony with others.

Spiritual liberty is not seen but it is experienced. Spiritual liberty is freedom from psychological and/or emotional bondage. Spiritual liberty is freedom from debilitating experiences like depression, worry, and/or anxiety. Many of these issues are chronic and require professional medical treatment, but spiritual liberty is also available through faith that can offer freedom from many of those unseen burdens of life. Moreover, spiritual liberty through faith can overcome the most difficult of circumstances due to physical bondage by providing peace of heart and calm to the soul. Spiritual liberty through faith overcomes fear because faith and fear cannot coexist. Faith displaces fear. Faith delivers spiritual liberty.

Spiritual liberty is a key component of faith according to scripture. "Now the Lord is the Spirit; and where the Spirit of the Lord is, there is liberty." (2 Corinthians 3:17) That is, scripture states that faith in Christ imparts liberty in the soul and life in the individual exercising that faith. Liberty is part of our new nature found in our faith. It is a critical component of our faith's DNA. Faith cannot effectively exist within the confines of our soul without experiencing some degree of liberty. Understanding the relationship between faith and liberty, we then realize suppressing liberty through slavery creates a conflict of faith in both the lives of the enslaved and the lives of those who support slavery. The acceptance of slavery during the days of Lincoln produced a crisis of faith that derailed our nation from its pursuit of liberty for all. A crisis of faith through a conflict in the souls of those in the faith communities of our nation affected the path of the entire nation.

This is not a unique phenomenon in the history of the people of faith. Scripture describes "the righteousness of God is revealed from faith to faith" (Romans 1:17). This characterizes the life of faith as an iterative process of figuring out how to live our faith in a practical manner. But the issue of liberty is such an integral part of our faith that we are told "to stand fast" in the liberty that we have experienced through our own faith experience, "by which Christ has made us free" (Galatians 5:1). We are additionally warned that we are "called to liberty" and not to use it for our own "opportunity" of gain but use our liberty "to serve" others (Galatians 5:13). In other words, the defense of our own liberty and the advancement of liberty in the lives of others through faith is a key component of our life of faith. We are given the liberty to love one another and serve each other.

It is easy for us to judge the faith communities of years ago because we have no understanding of the context of their lives or the pressures of living during those days. All I know is that we struggle immensely with living a life of faith today with all the pressures of life and living in our modern world. My purpose in this discussion is not to condemn anyone for living out their life of faith according to their own convictions. Rather, my purpose is to try to understand the challenges then and how they relate to and implicate the life of faith we try to live today in our still imperfect union.

LIBERTY FOR SOME IS NOT LIBERTY AT ALL

In our own experience, we know that partial liberty means to be restricted from the total liberty experience. We have the liberty to move freely throughout our nation anywhere within the confines of its borders. In so doing, we have a lot of liberty. Were our passports revoked, however, our liberty would be constrained, we would not experience the beauty in the world outside the borders of our nation. That is a life of some liberty, not complete liberty.

If we were confined to those conditions and had no knowledge of other lands, that probably would not seem so bad to us. But if we saw or were told of others traveling across the ocean and enjoying the total splendor of the world, we would be resentful, angry, and desire to be free.

Now imagine being so constrained in our life that we are told where to live, whom to live with, what food to eat, and what labor to do and are punished physically while enduring that lack of freedom. And in plain sight, while enduring our enslavement we saw others completely free. That would be torturous. That is not a united nation. It is a nation divided by its liberty. History tells us that a nation divided by liberty is destined to be a nation that eventually physically divides.

What was true in our nation during the days of Lincoln is true today. A nation divided by its liberty is a nation that is not a united nation and is destined to be physically divided. The solution to that dilemma is to provide the same liberty for all people. Liberty should not be subject to race, religion, or politics. Rather, the solution is one nation under God with liberty for all.

CHAPTER 4

The Decision to Divide

There is nothing more exciting in our lives than welcoming a newborn into our families. My wife and I recently experienced the arrival of our third grandchild. This baby girl is enthralling to watch as each day she grows and becomes more and more aware of the world around her. Equally rewarding is witnessing a daughter become a mother and a son become a father. By some divine orchestration, an inherent change moves these two young adults to become laser-focused on nurturing this little bundle of joy. Seemingly, just a few days ago career moves, financial obligations, and a daily routine of anything but parenting filled their lives. Now, this couple has immediately become intently focused on the welfare of their infant daughter.

As my wife and I witness this transformation of two uniting to become three and possibly more someday, we want to exhort them to enjoy every moment of this season for it will quickly pass. In what seems to be a blink of an eye, this baby will approach adolescence and her eventual own independent life journey. "Therefore, a man shall leave his father and mother and be joined to his wife, and they shall become one flesh." (Genesis 2:24) This scriptural principle does not mandate that this little girl be destined for marriage, but it does allude to the day that she too will eventually leave her parent's home as she is launched into life. It is only when you reach an age approximate to mine that you realize that "life is like a vapor that quickly vanishes." (James 4:14)

It is in the natural order of life for relationships to develop and to divide. This occurs in the lives of people, families, marriages, businesses, organizations, states, and sometimes entire nations. When division occurs, in most cases it is predictable and deliberate— predictable because all the indications of division exist within the relationship long before the act occurs and deliberate because it requires a final decision to act before anything is done. In many instances, absolutes and absolutism are key components of the decision to divide. Such was the case when our nation was divided through the Civil War.

ABSOLUTES AND ABSOLUTISM

Absolutes are in all phases of our lives. Absolutes are pure and free from any mixture. *Absolute* is a word that implies no exception or alternative to what is being described. The longer we live, the older we become and look. That is an absolute. All of us must eat and drink a requisite amount to sustain life, or we will not survive. That is also an absolute.

Absolutism is when an absolute standard or principal rules in a body or absolute power is vested in an authority. For example, in my granddaughter's Taekwondo school, her Zen master is the absolute authority in determining if a student is qualified to advance to the next belt. In order to progress, each student must master a variety of kicks and punches. Additionally, the Zen master must receive verbal confirmation from a parent that the student is submissive to parental authority and doing well in their schoolwork. These are the rules of the class, with no exceptions. The Zen master is the absolute authority. That is absolutism.

Absolutism exists in a nation when factions develop that hold social, political, or civil positions that are without compromise. During the Civil War era, factions developed in our nation in all three of these areas. The compelling issue of the divide was slavery. The binding element of the factions was the merger of faith and politics.

The divisive issue of slavery took root on opposite sides of our nation's political structure. That divide was accelerated when the faith communities became polarized. That is, the faith communities divided into opposing political positions with no intent to compromise. This divide occurred while sharing the same faith and the same biblical authority. This social, religious, and political divide then escalated into a civil divide through the act of secession and the initiation of a war between the states.

THE POLITICAL ABSOLUTES OF THE TIMES

Although I am neither a historian nor a political scientist, I can share anecdotal evidence describing the environment in Civil War times that has been published in various sources. A good start is the contrast in views of the two political leaders of the times, Lincoln (Republican) and Steven Douglas (Democrat).

Steven Douglas who won the race against Lincoln for an Illinois state senate seat, considered the negro race incapable of self-government. His position proposed slavery as a charitable response. In this case, slavery was viewed as being similar to those services provided for the blind, the deaf and mute, or the insane.

Lincoln's point of view differed decidedly from Douglas's. Looking at the north-south divide in practices of slavery in which slavery was considered right and just to the south and wrong and immoral to the north, he demurred at this division being merely situationally bound practices. He asserted that right and wrong were higher-order (moral) realities and not situationally dictated.

The political posture of entities within the nation gravitated toward one of two sides—pro or anti-slavery. Much like the political landscape in our nation today, no political alternatives were proposed.

THE ABSOLUTES OF FAITH COMMUNITIES

For a faith community to embrace a position on a social issue, the position must agree with the doctrinal tenets of that faith community. All faith communities look toward their faith leaders to guide them in the acceptance of any social position and its suitability to their doctrines of faith.

For example, I was a practicing Catholic for the first 30 years of my life. Then and now, the Catholic Church's position on birth control is natural family planning. At that time, I believed any other practice of birth control would be a violation of my faith and a sin. When I left the Catholic Church, birth control was no longer an issue of my faith because I no longer submitted to the Catholic Church leaders as the authorities governing my moral decisions.

To trace the history of how and when the Christian leaders of the Civil War era transitioned to a full-throated defense of slavery is well beyond the scope of this writing. Simply described positions of ministers varied greatly. Some were hypocritical. For example, it was common for ministers to take a hard line against slavery from the pulpit while personally owning slaves. Some declared that the abolition spirit was undeniably atheistic. While others were zealots against the cause of slavery like the famous John Brown who died because of his resistance to slavery. Suffice it to say that at this point, the faith communities were aligned on one side of the social issue of the times or the other, largely based on the interpretation of their respective denominational leaders. That is a part of our nation's history and was destined to be repeated as recently as 30 years ago. That is a subject to be visited in part two of this book.

Faith communities simply aligning on one particular side of a social issue is not fatal to the functioning of a nation, but when large segments of a faith community align with a political party exclusively, a new dynamic seems to take hold in a nation. That alignment of faith and politics manifests a position that quickly becomes absolute. That is, the merging of faith and politics seems to diminish the spirit of compromise.

This can be attributed to the belief that this union has the blessing of God, while the opposing position does not.

Once a nation is immersed in this type of division it is open to any catalyst that may easily increase the gap between the opposing positions. In a democracy like ours, the effectiveness of governance is based on the balance of the three branches of government. That is, the Executive, Legislative, and Judicial branches complement each other to provide a balanced operation of government. If one branch gets out of line, so to speak, the other two branches work together to restore balance. One branch can take a decisive action that will temporarily cause some instability, but the design is to restore balance over time. In times of deep national divide, like that of an impending Civil War, radical action by the Judicial branch can facilitate an acceleration of division in the country, plummeting the nation into crisis. That is exactly what happened with the Supreme Court's Dred Scott Decision.

THE DRED SCOTT CASE

The Dred Scott case was a decade-long fight for the freedom of an enslaved black man. Born into slavery in Virginia around 1799, he moved with his owner to the slave state of Alabama and then to Missouri by the time he was 30 years old. A new owner moved Dred to the free state of Illinois and then to Wisconsin Territory where slavery was outlawed. Several moves and several owners occurred over the following years while Dred Scott met and married Harriet Robinson and had two children. After their marriage in a rare civil ceremony, the ownership of Harriet was transferred to Dred Scott's owner, Dr. John Emerson, an army surgeon.

The Scott family moved with their owner as he changed assignments. They never tried to run away or sue for freedom while living in or traveling through free states and territories. In 1843, John Emerson died suddenly, and the Scotts became his wife Irene's property. Scott tried multiple times to purchase his freedom from Irene, but she refused.

In April 1846, Dred and Harriet filed lawsuits for freedom in St. Louis, Missouri. Initially, they were denied their freedom on a technicality but won it on a retrial in 1850. The case was appealed to the Missouri Supreme Court which reversed the lower court's decision in 1852, again enslaving Dred Scott and his family.[23]

In 1856, the case made its way to the U.S. Supreme Court. The decision was taken in March 1857, by a seven-to-two vote, that the Declaration of Independence's assertion of equality did not include Black people. The ruling went on to say that Black people were not citizens and that any future restrictions on slavery were unconstitutional. The Supreme Court, referred to as the Taney Court, was trying to resolve the political and social issues of their time with a single blow, a ruling from the highest court in the land. Similar to what we see today from our Supreme Court making rulings that greatly influence social and political issues of our times.

History.com describes the impact of the Dred Scott decision on the Civil War as follows. "The Dred Scott Decision outraged abolitionists, who saw the Supreme Court's ruling as a way to stop the debate about slavery in the territories. The divide between the North and South over slavery grew and culminated in the secession of Southern states from the Union and the creation of the Confederate States of America."[24]

IN SEARCH OF A COMPROMISE

This was the political, judicial, and social climate of our nation when Lincoln was asked and accepted to be a candidate for the presidency in the upcoming election for the Republican party. On Monday, February 27, 1860, Lincoln made his first speech as a presidential candidate at Cooper Union in New York City.

Lincoln made the case that the founding fathers of our nation framed a constitution to prevent the spread of slavery. Lincoln said,

> This is all Republicans ask—all Republicans desire—in relation to slavery, as those fathers marked it, so let it

23. https://www.history.com/topics/black-history/dred-scott-case
24. *Dred Scott Case.* Downloaded from https://history.com/black-history/dred-scott-case August 4, 2024

be marked again, as an evil not to be extended, but to be tolerated and protected only because of and so far as its actual presence among us makes that toleration and protection a necessity. Let all the guarantees those fathers gave it, be, not grudgingly, but fully and fairly maintained.[25]

In other words, slavery could remain only in those states where it currently existed without any future expansion.

Lincoln was not reversing his position on slavery. Competing for the highest political office in the nation changed his view from advocating a position on the social issue of slavery to a position on addressing a solution to that social issue. He was already thinking like a president by searching for a solution to the problem that was dividing the nation. In that, he was no longer representing a portion of the nation's people but trying to think how to better represent all of the nation's people. That is the difference between a politician and a leader. Unfortunately, many of our elected officials are only politicians.

Lincoln continued,

I do not mean to say we are bound to follow implicitly in whatever our fathers did. To do so, would be to discard all the lights of current experience—to reject all progress— all improvement. What I do say is, that if we would supplant the opinions and policy of our fathers in any case, we should do so upon evidence so conclusive, and argument so clear, that even their great authority, fairly considered and weighed, cannot stand."[26]

Lincoln knew the solution was a compromise that would be the result of lessons learned as the nation grew in its experience with slavery and the requisite knowledge from that experience. In that experience, a clear,

---

25. *And There Was Light* by Jon Meacham, P.182; Random House, 2022.
26. *And There Was Light* by Jon Meacham, P.182; Random House, 2022.

fair, and conclusive compromise could be reached. But Lincoln also knew there was no such argument to be made with regard to the expansion of slavery. Given where the nation was at this point in time, there was no compromise to be had.

No relationship is perfect. No matter how closely aligned two entities are, there will always be disagreements, differences of opinion, and conflicts. This is true in marriages, families, businesses, churches, and certainly nations. When the ability to compromise is lost, then that relationship has entered into absolutism. Where absolutism exists in a relationship, the relationship becomes dysfunctional. When absolutism occurs in a democracy, the democracy dies and begins moving toward an autocracy. It was true in the days of Lincoln. It is true today.

ABSOLUTISM DIVIDES A NATION

Lincoln was well aware that the South would never compromise on the limiting of slavery to the current states. The prevailing thought in the South was that only the expansion of slavery to other states, territories, and areas beyond our nation would ensure slavery's future.

As the Democratic National Committee called the party's 1860 convention to order in Charleston, South Carolina the delegates fell into procedural squabbles immediately. William Lowndes Yancy of Alabama represented the opinion of the white Southerners, who wanted to yield not an inch, feeling that their honor was at stake.

At that point, our nation was given over to absolutism. Two segments of our nation were irrevocably divided with no hope of compromise. History tells us the Civil War was only months away at this point.

FAITH AND POLITICS: A TOXIC BLEND

I recently had the pleasure of reuniting with the former worship leader of the church I pastored many years ago. Before our get-together, we previously had only two brief conversations in many years. Our recent meeting was designated as a time to catch up on all the events in our lives since we had last seen each other over two decades ago. The visit was wonderful as we casually sat in his living room, recounting some precious memories and learning about the more recent details of our lives. As we sat down for the evening meal, the discussion turned to politics. What followed was completely unexpected for all of us.

I am not sure what was said that prompted me to ask which candidate he had supported in the last presidential election. From that moment on, the conversation took on a completely different spirit. What filled the environment of the day up to that moment was a feeling of mutual respect and alignment of common core beliefs that governed each of our lives. What emerged was an emotional, political discussion that quickly broke down into defensive arguments for our respective positions. It was a dramatic illustration of how two who shared the same faith could be politically polarized without any hope of establishing a compromising middle ground between us.

I am sad to say the visit ended abruptly after dinner because of our political differences. There was a tension introduced into our dinner conversation that affected the spirit of the visit. We suddenly realized that two people who had so much in common laboring in our faith together many years ago were now different. Our decidedly different views soured the sweet savor of our relationship. Suddenly, we were not as comfortable with each other. The relationship that we had cherished changed. The old relationship that we remembered was replaced by a worldview shaped by recent political and social events. We parted as friends, with handshakes and hugs, but I was brokenhearted for days afterward as a result.

I am sad to say that in my experience, this relationship dynamic has reoccurred over recent years with both long-time friends and family members. This has affirmed my belief that the mixing of faith and politics is a toxic blend that divides relationships. It is toxic enough to divide families, communities, and an entire nation. That was true during the Civil War era, and it is true today.

So, what is one to do in these circumstances? The first thing we must learn to understand is that there lies a divine purpose behind every decision to divide.

THE DIVINE PURPOSE BEHIND THE DIVIDE

Scripture designates King Solomon (David's son) as the wisest man who lived (1 Kings 4:29-31). He penned the book of Ecclesiastes which states "To everything there is a season, A time for every purpose under heaven" (Ecclesiastes 3:1) which was the subject of a popular song released in 1965 by the Byrds called "Turn, Turn, Turn." Solomon continues in his writing to list a series of events under God's sovereignty that reinforce the premise of his writing that there is a season for everything. In verse three, Solomon's list includes "A time to break down and a time to build up." What is declared in scripture is that God sovereignly reserves the right to "break down" and "build up" to achieve His divine purposes. I believe this includes all relationships, including marriages, families, businesses, churches, governments, and even nations. Some clerics believe this is God's pattern of spiritual transformation.

Richard Rohr, a Franciscan priest and a globally recognized ecumenical teacher, states, "We grow by passing beyond some perfect order, through a usually painful and seemingly unnecessary disorder, to an enlightened reorder or "resurrection." This is the "pattern that connects" and solidifies our relationship with everything around us. To grow toward love, union, salvation, or enlightenment (I use the words almost interchangeably), we must be moved from *Order* to *Disorder* and then ultimately to *Reorder*."[27]

There was a time in my faith journey when I would have dismissed any concept of divine Order, Disorder, and Reorder as Rohr suggests as pure mysticism that has no place in my Christian faith. Fortunately for me, I had already experienced what Rohr describes many years before I read Rohr's work. I know this to be true in my life, and it was a catalyst for my first writing. I write about that faith experience and call it "A Wilderness Experience."[28] It was not until I read Rohr's work that I became aware of any teaching about how God is sovereign in these events of our lives.

---

27. *The Universal Christ* by Richard Rohr, P. 243-244; Convergent Books, 2019.
28. *The Evidence of Things Unseen* by Jerry Aveta, P.43; West Bow Press, 2021.

I offer that concept as an explanation of how God can work in the middle of a catastrophic event like the Civil War. The evidence in my own life was the experience of going from Order to Disorder to Reorder in my married life, transforming my faith. The experience in our nation's history was going from Order to Disorder to Reorder through a civil war to eliminate slavery.

I believe God is using these methods as I pen these words today in our nation and throughout the world. Around the world, various nations like Ukraine and Israel are in various stages of physical and governmental transitions. In our own nation, the boundaries of norms are being tested in its governance and the legal interpretation of its limits. There is no reason to believe that God will depart from these methods of Order, Disorder, and Reorder in the future. The only question is will we learn from those experiences? That will be the subject later in this book.

CHAPTER 5

The Pathology
of Violence

I grew up in a small town in Central New Jersey about two hours west of New York City, one hour east of Philadelphia, and 45 minutes north of Trenton. I would see on the nightly news stories of robberies, homicides, and other violent crimes routinely occurring in those cities. I lived in that town until I graduated from college and can honestly say I do not recall any act of violence occurring or being reported in the local paper as long as I lived there. I am sure violence existed, but it was not part of my routine life experience. I was not aware of violent crimes or demonstrations being part of my daily living. It was not until many years later that I witnessed a violent beating during the course of my daily routine.

Teaching high school math on the eastern shore of Virginia offered me many new life experiences. Island living provided opportunities such as unlimited boating, fishing, swimming in the ocean, and surviving two hurricanes. Teaching in a local mainland public school afforded me the opportunity to witness a physical assault in my classroom.

One student, considerably larger than the other, disagreed with what was said or not said as each entered the classroom on what was a routine day. I was engaged in my hall monitoring and greeting the students at the door when I heard a disturbance in the classroom. As I turned to enter the room, I couldn't believe my eyes. The larger boy was straddling the smaller boy on the floor, delivering blows with his fists to the pinned boy's face. The smaller boy was helplessly trying to fend off the blows without much success. Blood was flying everywhere. Some students were screaming, and others were staring as they witnessed this terrorizing scene.

I was eventually summonsed to court to testify about the events of that day. The larger boy was sent off to some sort of reform school for a while. A few months later, he was back in my class with the same boy he had beaten and the same students who had witnessed the assault. It was business as usual for these kids. For me, that class was never the same. From the day of the incident, I dreaded going to that class. While trying to teach, I was on constant vigil for any sign of an emerging conflict, fearing a reoccurrence of the events that day. It was the most violent scene I ever witnessed in all my years. And it happened in a ninth-grade Algebra class.

I lost track of the boy who incited the violence that day. I believe it was sometime during the next school year when that same boy was the subject of discussion in the teachers' lounge. He was the police's prime suspect in the setting of a fire to the trailer where he lived with his sister and mother. The boy and sister escaped through a window, leaving his mother and boyfriend victimized by the fire while asleep.

How do children become so accustomed to violence that they easily resort to it as part of their daily experience? What is their path to such violence? I am sure there are many reasons, some obvious even to a math teacher with no personal experience with matters like this. Most of the reasons are hidden from view in the daily life of the child. They are experiences that have occurred throughout his or her life, varying in degree and frequency. Those causes are deeply embedded into the life experience, perhaps going back generations. It can only take the skill of a talented psychologist, doctor, or social worker to begin to identify the root causes of violence in a child. Even with the skills of these talented people, it is my belief those deep-rooted issues can only be healed by Divine intervention. It takes one of those intersections of the natural (us) with the supernatural (God).[29]

The pathology that leads a nation to civil war is filled with violence as well. Violence that is similar but different from that of a child. Similar in the sense it may be years in development before breaking out into a civil war among the people of a nation. Different in the sense that the violent steps leading to civil war are in the open, publicly committed, and recorded by history. Such is the case in the history of our nation's violence leading to the Civil War.

As mentioned previously, Minute Men militias modeled after the Revolutionary patriots began in the South as early as the 1830s. These militias, mainly comprised of white plantation owners, were part of an organized radical secessionist group to build support for Southern independence. Barbara Walter states, "Civil war is sometimes traced to a single incident: a trigger. Sometimes it's an election, sometimes a failed protest, sometimes a natural disaster."[30] In this case, after years of organizing, the South was ready for a post-election civil war.

THE ELECTION OF A PRESIDENT

The election of the President of the United States is a time-honored tradition governed by our Constitution and is usually held in high regard by most of the citizens of our nation. However, there have been cases in our history when this critical element of the democratic process of our country has been exploited to alter the outcome illegally and violently. Such was the case with the election of Abraham Lincoln.

As the election of 1860 drew close, history describes our nation as a political volcano ready to spill over into violence. It was believed at the time that the issue of slavery was ready to sever the Union and that Lincoln's

---

29. *The Evidence of Things Unseen* by Jerry Aveta; P. xvii-xviii; West Bow Press, 2021.
30. *How Civil Wars Start* by Barbara F. Walter; P.96; Crown Publishers, New York; 2022.

election was considered the prime instigator of the divide. This was the case even though when Lincoln spoke of slavery it was with his repeated assurances that he would not interfere with it wherever it already existed. Reports of young men in Virginia bound by solemn oaths to assassinate Lincoln if elected were dismissed as just talk. However, reportedly death was on Lincoln's mind as these threats reached Springfield, where Lincoln was residing at the time of the election.

It is true today that the media plays a vital role in capturing the mood of our nation leading up to the election of our president. At the time of this writing, we are a few months away from the next presidential election, and the news networks are filled with routine polls capturing the mood of the nation. The same was true leading up to Lincoln's election. One of the popular newspapers of the times, *The New York Herald,* wrote about anticipated actions and the subsequent violence based on the election outcomes. Stories about the wholesale liberation of slaves and the burning of the fields with the dwellings of their masters. Anticipated massacres of both old and young produced a state of fear. Talk of violence filled the air.

A similar phenomenon exists today. Some people refuse to accept the facts of an issue regardless of the proof presented or how many times it is explained. For example, the most recent presidential election in our nation was fueled with controversy over it being a fair election. Some declare the election was stolen through cheating and illegitimate voting methods. Despite the overwhelming documentation that these are false claims and over 60 court decisions affirming the election was fair, many in our nation refuse to believe it. Large swaths of support still exist today, several years later, for any candidate who maintains that the last election was stolen. Just as in the days of Lincoln, truth doesn't necessarily matter in the political position of some.

On Tuesday, November 6, 1860, Abraham Lincoln was elected President of the United States by the slimmest of margins. He barely won the popular vote by less than a 54% majority in 18 states. He won only 2.1 percent of the votes in slave states. His name was not even on the ballot in 10 other states.

Lincoln was certainly not the first president to have been elected by a slim margin, and time has proven that he was not the last. Just a few years ago, we had the outcome of a presidential election determined by the number of "hanging chads" counted in the state of Florida. It required a Supreme Court decision to determine the outcome of that election. It was the case then as it was in the days of Lincoln. The president-elect represents the entire nation regardless of how slim the margin of victory is. In those instances, there are many upset with the outcome. Such was the case in the days of Lincoln,

REACTIONS TO AN ELECTION

Less than a week after the presidential election, South Carolina's two United States senators resigned their seats in Congress. The state called for a secession convention to meet in Columbia on Monday, December 17. December 20, 1860, the South Carolina state convention passed an ordinance to secede from the Union by a unanimous vote. Mississippi, Louisiana, Florida, Alabama, Georgia, and Texas followed over the next six weeks with additional states following soon after.

The effigies of Lincoln were often burned in demonstrations against the Union throughout the southern states. The only time I have witnessed something being burned in effigy was the mascot of an opposing football team the night before a big game. That experience intended to unify all the supporters to cheer our hearts out for our team during the big game. It invoked a spirit of team pride to promote a competitive game that hopefully would be in our favor. It was never construed to be an act of violence, rebellion, or animus.

This was not the case in Lincoln's days. Burning a political figure in effigy as the result of an election has never been a consideration in my experience, and I believe the same is true for most people in our nation. There have been violent demonstrations for many other reasons, but I never imagined a violent demonstration could occur in our nation over the result of a political election, especially a presidential election.

All that changed in our nation on January 6, 2021. While no images were burned in effigy that day, what we witnessed was a peaceful political gathering whipped up into a violent frenzy that resulted in untold damage to the U.S. Capitol and several lives being lost. While the prosecution of the perpetrators on the Capitol that day is ongoing as of this writing, the lesson learned is that civil violence is just a political rally away in our nation today.

What occurred during the days following Lincoln's election was similar to the events of January 6, 2021, experienced on Capitol Hill. Both events recognized that the most vulnerable time during the formal transfer of power from one administration to the next is during the count of the electoral votes from the election.

January 6, the plan included a rally at the White House and a march down Pennsylvania Avenue with the target of interrupting the electoral count ongoing during the joint session of Congress on Capitol Hill. In the days of Lincoln, the process of the electoral count was more public and consequently more vulnerable.

TAKING THE CAPITOL- STOPPING THE COUNT

In the days before Lincoln's inauguration, the Washington area was filled with rumors of insurrection. Having lived and worked in the Washington D.C. area for most of my adult life, I can testify that the area encompasses a political environment like none other. People who work in the highest levels of our government walk the city streets and interact with the general population of the area. The local media is dominated by the politics of the day like nowhere else in our nation. Granted today's political environment in the D.C. area is unlike the days of Lincoln but similar in the prognostication of political events and the endless stream of rumors in the air.

Rumors of Armies marching on the city to stop the transfer of power were rampant. Even Lincoln realized the greatest vulnerability to delay the events was during the certification of the election. In other words, disrupting the count of the electoral votes was the easiest way to stop Lincoln from taking office.

The insurrection never occurred, and the certification of Lincoln's election was not delayed largely because of the actions of two individual patriots, Winfield Scott, and John Breckinridge.

Winfield Scott, the commanding general of the U.S. Army, acting to preserve the Union and prevent an obstruction of the electoral count, deployed federal troops throughout the capital.

As for John Breckinridge, he was responsible for the transfer of the Electoral College votes from the Senate to the House, where he presided and certified the election. Although he was defeated for president and sympathetic to the Southern cause, Breckinridge did his duty and thereby saved the nation.

At this point, we must reflect on the uncanny similarity between the events described in this chapter and those transpiring in January 2021. On that day, our democracy survived an assault by a group of citizens dissatisfied with the election results. The intent was the same as during Lincoln's time: stop the count of the electoral votes and delay the inauguration of the president-elect. Once again, this effort was stopped only by the courage of those appointed to defend the Capitol (the Capitol Police) and the integrity of the sitting Vice-President of our nation. Once again, our nation was saved.

I think it is important to dwell on that point: our nation was saved in that moment. Saved from what? Saved from chaos, for sure. Saved from an unprecedented sequence of events for which there is no constitutional road map. That means our country would have been subject to being led by one person. At that point, we would no longer be a democracy, a country led by its people, but rather an autocracy, a country led by one person.

Autocrats are generally interested in their own agenda as opposed to following the will of the people as in a democracy. All we have to do is look at the experiences of countries like China, North Korea, and Russia to understand how an autocratic ruler behaves. That should give us some insight when determining our choice in future elections. Any politician who has previously demonstrated autocratic tendencies should no longer be considered a viable option to be president of our democratic nation.

Just as in the days of Lincoln, there are factions in our nation today that do not agree with this thinking. So, we as a nation continue on this path of history repeating itself. We have not learned from the past, even a past as recent as a few years ago. It remains to be seen where our inability to learn from history will take our nation.

AN APPEAL TO OUR BETTER ANGELS

Shortly after noon on Monday, March 4, 1861, Abraham Lincoln rode in an open carriage up Pennsylvania Avenue accompanied by President Buchanon. They were bound for the Senate chamber where Hannibal Hamlin would be sworn in as vice president. They would then proceed to the covered platform that had been erected on the East front of the Capitol for the presidential inauguration. Escorting the procession were double files of cavalrymen. Sharpshooters were stationed on rooftops along the avenue. Orders were ordered to watch the windows and fire upon them in case any attempt should be made to fire upon the Presidential carriage.

The task that Lincoln faced was formidable. Sixty percent of the voters the previous fall had supported other candidates. The degree and force of the nation's divisions had never been more profound. Much of the South was either in secession or contemplating it. The South was where it was because it believed the North, embodied by Lincoln, held it in moral contempt. Antislavery was viewed as a "religion of hate" based on the Northern crusade aimed at the sin of Southern slavery. The South believed that measures to restrict slavery to its existing realm were a denial of equal rights and implied a pretension of moral superiority.

Lincoln tried to calm the fears of the South in his inaugural address. He first cited his record to declare "no purpose, directly or indirectly, to interfere with the institution of slavery in the States where it exists. I believe I have no lawful right to do so, and I have no inclination to do so."[31] But Lincoln's First Inaugural is often remembered for its closing appeal.

> "We are not enemies, but friends. We must not be enemies. Though passion may have strained, it must not break our bonds of affection. The mystic chords of memory, stretching from every battlefield, and patriot grave, to every living heart and hearthstone, all over this broad land, will yet swell the chorus of the Union, when again touched, as surely they will be, ***by the better angels of our nature***."[32]

Lincoln's reference to our "better angels" refers to the "light" that is in each of us. The side that resides opposite that dark place to which we all retreat at times. When I am operating in the "light" my wife refers to it "as my best self," and I know exactly what she means. When I am operating in the light, I am patient, in pursuit of understanding my relationships in a better way and looking for common ground in the areas where we disagree. This is what I believe Lincoln was imploring the people of the divided nation he had just been elected to do.

I believe our nation today is in desperate need of hearing that message again. However, I am afraid that if such a message were to resound throughout our country today, the result would be similar to the result when Lincoln proclaimed it. It was largely ignored, and the nation went to war.

THE FIRING ON FT. SUMTER

Walking into the White House office the morning after his inauguration, Lincoln was startled by news from Fort Sumter's commanding officer, who reported that the soldiers at the fort would face starvation in approximately a month because supplies had been cut off by the Confederate forces. The

---

31. *Lincoln's First Inaugural Address.* Downloaded from https://www.battlefields.org/;earn/primary-sources/lincolns-first-inaugural-address, July 29, 2024.

32. Ibid, P. 233

secession up to this point had been largely a peaceable crisis. All that was about to change. After much deliberation, Lincoln decided he wanted Ft. Sumter resupplied. Confederate commissioners sent word there were to be no negotiations. Just before dawn on the morning of Friday, April 12, 1861, the first shots were fired on Ft. Sumter from Confederate batteries. "The last ray of hope for preserving the Union peaceably expired at the assault upon Ft. Sumter," Lincoln remarked in his 1861 State of the Union Address.[33] War had come.

Several years ago, my wife and I had the opportunity to visit Ft. Sumter long before the notion of writing this book ever occurred to me. At that time, I did not appreciate the gravity of the moment. If I were to visit there again, I believe I would now get a sense of the history of that place. It is a relatively small island close to the shore. What remains of the fortress does not seem nearly enough to protect the soldiers occupying their duty station. What was probably viewed as a scenic, serene location to serve one's military duty was turned into a nightmare that early dawn in April 1861. It is only in those moments of losing our liberty do we often learn to appreciate what we once had and took for granted.

Scholars know where civil wars tend to break out and who tends to start them. But what triggers the event? What brings people to the place where they feel there is no option other than to fight? Walter asks and suggests,

> What finally tips a country into conflict? Citizens can absorb a lot of pain. They will accept years of discrimination and poverty and remain quiet, enduring the ache of slow decline. What they can't take is the loss of hope. It is when a group looks into the future and sees nothing but additional pain that they start to see violence as their only path to progress.[34]

---

33. *Abraham Lincoln's 1862 Annual Message to Congress.* Downloaded from American Battlefield Trust: https://www.battlefields.org/learn/primary-sources/abraham-lincolns-1862-annual-message-congress-final-remarks.

34. "How Civil Wars Start" by Barbara F. Walter, P.84; Crown publishers;2022.

Such was the case after Lincoln's election. Slave owners and their advocates in the South felt morally judged and politically cornered. They no longer believed in their elected officials and thought all that they had personally worked for and materially achieved was at risk. What is more, they believed God was on their side. That is a dangerous combination of emotions: fear of the future and a moral imperative to act. A simple Google search tells us (History.com; statista.com) that an estimated 620,000 lives were lost in the war that ensued. It was the deadliest of all American wars. It caused more fatalities than all the other wars combined.

SOME CONCLUDING THOUGHTS

I am not a theologian nor a bible scholar. I am simply a teacher with a pastor's heart who has spent many years ministering in many different types of denominational churches, including my own which I started and closed after seven years. I have ministered in large and small churches. I have taught many different classes under the auspices of different churches, sacred and secular schools, and various settings. I have counseled groups, couples, and singles. I have been with some during their last moments on earth. I have endeavored to invite God into the middle of all those activities. At times, I have sensed an overpowering presence of God, but on many occasions I have not; yet I am always looking for some sense of God's approval. After 30+ years of experience, I can honestly say there were far more times that God was silent on a matter than there were of His confirmation. But what I have learned from the entirety of that labor is the certainty to recognize when God has surrendered us over to the fruit of our own labor. That is, those moments when we find ourselves in circumstances that are more a result of our own efforts than God's divine direction in our lives.

I believe the Civil War was such an event. Evidence of that is both sides were claiming God to be on their side. Both sides used the same biblical authority but reached different conclusions. Each side would claim the other is misinterpreting the intent of scripture, offering a different contextual interpretation, or simply stating the other is wrong. How can there be such confusion in communities of faith under the same authority of God? The answer is that neither is operating under God's authority, but each is striving under their efforts. "For God is not the author of confusion but of peace, as in all the churches of the saints" (1 Corinthians 14:33). Faith mandates communities of faith to find common ground. The confronting issue of those times was that faith was intertwined with politics. That created a volatile dynamic.

The irony is we are experiencing that same volatile dynamic in our nation today. The toxic blend of faith and politics has fueled division in our nation's faith communities and the nation at large. We are witnessing the same type of divide over the social issues of the day. That is, faith communities use the same biblical authority on opposite sides of the same social issue.

Part two of this book addresses those issues of today, drawing the comparison to the days of Lincoln.

PART 2

WHEN LIBERTY

ENSLAVES:

A CASE STUDY

CHAPTER 6

An Overview of
Times Present

Back to the Future is a 1985 movie describing the adventures of a teenager played by Michael J. Fox who uses a time-traveling DeLorean automobile built by his friend scientist to travel back and forth 30 years in time. If I had access to a similar vehicle, I would love to hop in it and travel back 30 years into my life experience. If I did so, I would find myself at the beginning of what I refer to as my "bubble" years. The term refers to approximately 30 years when I was totally immersed in a life of faith among evangelical Christian churches.

I refer to these years as living in a "bubble" because they involved all aspects of the life of the church of which I was a member at the time. This included attending personal classes learning about my faith, teaching others who were new in the faith, and serving in various ministries, counseling, and leadership positions. This amounted to being at the church several nights a week and at multiple services on Sundays. If you add these activities to working 40+ hours a week, commuting several hours a day in the Washington D.C. area, and the requisite family time each day, there is not a lot of time for anything else. There was seldom time to keep up with daily news and/or current events. Political developments were of little or no significance to me. Consequently, life felt like living isolated in a "bubble."

There was no regret then or now for that lifestyle because I loved learning about the things of God and received great satisfaction in the service of my faith. However, if I could climb into a DeLorean automobile and travel back to those days, I would warn the people around me of the ongoing actions that create the dilemmas that the communities of faith face today, 30 years later.

FAITH AND POLITICS

If I had stepped out of my time-traveling Delorian 30 years ago, I would have stepped into what were the initial efforts of politicizing faith communities that have led to the polarization we see in those communities today. Unfortunately, I was not sufficiently politically astute or sufficiently mature in my faith to recognize the conflation of the two even though it was right in front of my eyes.

At that time, I was deeply involved with an independent Baptist church affiliated with Jerry Falwell (Sr.) Ministries. My pastor had been part of the first graduating class of what then was Lynchburg Baptist College and later became Liberty University. Jerry Falwell Sr. was my pastor's pastor. Jerry Falwell had visited our church in Alexandria, Virginia many times while I was a member. Our church hosted a satellite Bible Institute hosted by Liberty University, and I was one of the first graduates of both the diploma and advanced diploma programs. I went on to complete a Master of Arts Degree in Biblical Studies with a minor in Counseling from Liberty University. I met Pastor Falwell personally one time and was a great admirer of him and what he had accomplished over the years.

During those days I was well aware of Jerry Falwell's entry onto the political scene with his founding of the political action group called the Moral Majority, which helped establish the religious right as a force in

American politics. It wasn't until recently that I came to better understand the entire spectrum of the political involvement of Jerry Falwell and his Moral Majority.

Another frequent visitor to the church I attended in those first days was a gentleman named Tim LaHaye. Falwell, LaHaye, and other evangelical leaders represented the Religious Right and were actively involved in influencing the results of the 1980 presidential election. Since the 1970s, the major goals of the coalition of organizations and individuals known as the Religious Right (aka Christian Right or New Christian Right), have been to (1) get conservative Protestants to participate in the political process, (2) bring them into the Republican party, and (3) elect social conservatives to public office.

FROM POLITICIZATION TO POLARIZATION OF FAITH

As discussed in Part 1 of this book, faith was intertwined with politics even back in the days of Lincoln. That is, even then our nation experienced a "politicization" of faith, which simply means faith was brought into the political process. What exists today is a maturing of that blending of faith and politics, producing a more advanced state of division called "polarization." Over the years, there has been a migration from "politicization" to "polarization." As a result, not only are faith communities more divided but also this transition has facilitated a wider divide in our nation at large.

In the summer of 1980, President Carter, an Evangelical Christian, organized a White House Conference on Families thinking that conservatives and liberals might come together in a common cause to strengthen and protect families. However, leading into the conference, it became apparent that common ground would be difficult to attain.

Conservatives championed the traditional model: an archetypal family headed by a white, heterosexual male breadwinner. Liberals proposed a more adaptive family model, one that allowed for single parents and gay men and women. Liberals looked to the government to support families. Conservatives opposed government interference and sought instead to protect families from moral erosion.[35]

Frustration grew for the conservatives attending the White House Conference when it became evident that their key issues of banning abortion, defending school prayer, and opposing gay rights were going to be excluded from any final recommendations. Conservative delegates walked out of the official conference in protest.

Carter was a born-again evangelical, a Sunday school teacher, and assumedly represented the key values of conservative Christians. However, the leaders of the Christian Right felt it was clear that he was not one of them on the issues that mattered most. With the 1980 election weeks away, they united in their efforts to unseat Carter.

In 1980, the election widely hailed as the moment the Christian Right came into its own, evangelical voters bypassed the candidate who shared their faith tradition in favor of the one whose image and rhetoric more closely aligned with their values and aspirations. Guided by preachers like Robison, Falwell, and LaHaye, 67 percent of white evangelical voters chose Reagan over Carter; just four years earlier, Carter had received 49 percent of the evangelical vote and 56 percent of the white Baptist vote…. From Reagan on, no Democrat would again win the majority white evangelical support or threaten the same. Evangelicals' loyalty to the Republican Party would continue to strengthen, and they would use their electoral clout to help define the Republican agenda for the generation to come.[36]

The politicization of faith had reached new levels. The trends of evangelical voting established with the election of Reagan developed into an identity-based loyalty. That is, voting no longer required a deep analysis of the issues of the various candidates. As an evangelical, an identity was established as a conservative and that meant voting Republican without much further thought. That type of behavior is the definition of "polarization." Voting becomes identity-based, highly loyal,

35. *Jesus and John Wayne* by Kristen Kobes Du Mez; P.100; Liveright Publishing Corp., 2020.
36. Ibid, P.106

and not easily changed. It was at that time when the political allegiance of evangelicals in our nation moved from being "politicized" to being "polarized," largely as a result of the influence of the efforts of the Moral Majority and the Religious Right. For the most part, that same political disposition exists in our nation today.

THE RELIGIOUS RIGHT VERSUS THE EXTREME RIGHT

What seemed to be an effective way to change the political outcome in our nation many years ago has exposed the methods and the message of our faith to new extremes. The Religious Right of the past could not have foreseen the advent of the Extreme Right of the present. The first was motivated to infuse a specific view of faith into the political outcome of our nation. The second is motivated to infuse a specific method of radicalization into the political outcome of our nation. In the process, the faith message has been at times conflated with radicalized methods. The net result is actions like the bombing of abortion clinics or storming of our nation's capital for the cause of faith. This is the result when faith is thrown into the same political blender that includes radical methods to achieve outcomes.

Cynthia Miller-Idriss is a professor of education and sociology at American University and has studied extremism worldwide. She has researched the emotional and intellectual aspects of radicalization and has found that key elements include

> the role of individual grievances related to perceived marginalization, disenfranchisement, or relative inequality; a sense of betrayal, anger, and shame; exposure to violence; or the desire for belonging, meaning, purpose, and engagement.[37]

Many extremist elements have been identified as motivating factors for some voters in recent elections. People encounter extremist

---

37. *"Hate in the Homeland"* by Cynthia Miller-Idriss, P.3, Princeton University Press, 2020.

messages in their daily lives, including many opportunities for everyday experiences like far-right coffee shops, the mixed martial arts (MMA) scene, college campuses, social media, and online spaces. As well, micro-communities like evangelical churches and gun shows are targeted areas of extremist views.

I am not suggesting that churches routinely harbor extremists plotting against our government in their fellowship of faith. I also am not implying that evangelical Christians are particularly vulnerable to exposure to extremist views. What I am suggesting is that because of the polarization of faith, there is a common political identity of both the Religious Right in the past and the Extreme Right in the present that seems to be having an impact on the evangelical church.[38] Some evangelical church leaders have noted that impact.

Russell Moore is an evangelical Christian theologian and minister. He is editor-in-chief of *Christianity Today* and previously served as president of the Southern Baptist Convention's Ethics & Religious Liberty Commission. Moore states

> The issues—political fusion with Trumpism, Christian nationalism, white-identity backlash, the dismissing of issues such as abuse as "social justice," secularism, and several others—are (some of them or all of them) dividing almost every church, almost every family, almost every friendship I know. Every institution— from the presidency to local churches to family dining room tables—seems to be in crisis, almost to the point of breakdown.[39]

Let me clarify in layman's terms. Moore is alluding to the effects of polarization in faith communities that have seemingly accelerated

---

38. The reference "Religious Right: refers to the politicization of the faith communities in the 1980s; "Extreme Right" refers to the part of the Republican Party that embraces Christian Nationalism, white identity backlash, and dismissing violence as "social justice." (See, e.g. Losing Our Religion" by Russell Moore; Penguin Random House/Sentinel, 2023.)

39. *Losing Our Religion* by Russell Moore; P. 11; Penguin Random House: Sentinel, 2023.

the division in almost every dimension of our nation's daily experience. The conflation of issues through the same political affiliation supported by both the Religious Right (i.e., banning abortion, opposing LGTBQ rights, and the support of unrestricted gun rights) and the Extreme Right (i.e., Christian nationalism, white-identity backlash, and dismissing violence as "social justice") has had a dramatic national impact.

Most of us are not familiar with terms like "Christian nationalism" or "white identity backlash." Simply put, the first refers to the belief that our nation was and/or should be a Christian nation. The second refers to the philosophy that the "white middle class" is being left behind economically and is not politically represented very well in our nation. These are key issues of the Extreme Right of the Republican Party. Some evangelicals agree with these perspectives, and some do not. They can be confusing issues within communities of faith.

As a denominational leader, Moore speaks in a context that is rarely offered to the church. He speaks from a perspective that most have never experienced. He continues,

> After a near-decade of American evangelical Christianity defined almost wholly in the public view with Trumpism or racism or the predatory sexual or financial or psychological power dynamics of countless leaders, the outside world didn't seem to be judging us by "secular" standards as by our own.[40]

To comment to any full extent on the issues described by Moore is far beyond the scope of this writing. The purpose of including Moore's perspective is to give a view of the effect polarization has had on the political landscape of our nation and the communities of faith. Specifically, Moore's last point about the church being judged by its standards has implicated evangelicals in a self-incriminating way. That is, the secular community no longer has to look any further than our hypocritical behavior to conclude our message is ineffective.

---

40. "Losing Our Religion" by Russell Moore; P. 11; Penguin Random House: Sentinel, 2023.

However, to suggest that polarization is unique to communities of faith would be misleading and not an accurate portrayal of the political dynamic in our nation over recent years. There have been cultural changes in our nation that have been trending for years and have facilitated the polarization in our nation.

CULTURAL CHANGES CAUSING POLARIZATION

When Jerry Falwell brought the Religious Right to national prominence, cultural changes were already beginning in our nation. As early as the 1960s, generational shifts created a moving away from a materialistic emphasis and toward quality-of-life concerns. Younger generations preferred an emphasis on self-expression and values, as opposed to economic and physical security. These trends continued through the 1970s causing the values of each political party's electorate to change. As a result, "the two major parties gradually shifted to become more homogeneous internally in their cultural positions and more polarized between parties."[41]

This shift in party structure is important to note for this writing. Part 1 described the Democratic Party, dominant in the southern portion of our nation and advocating slavery, while the North was Republican and antislavery. Now, more than one hundred years later we see Southern segregationists deserting the Democratic party and Democrats becoming steadily more consistently socially liberal. Similarly, Republicans have, over time, become more socially conservative, beginning from the days of Nixon and his efforts to appeal to Southern conservatives. This has presented us with an escalating generation gap in the American electorate, with younger members more socially liberal and drawn toward the Democratic party and older folks more socially conservative and drawn toward the GOP.

Today, our nation's political parties are in opposite political corners like they were during the days of Lincoln. If slavery existed today, it is

---

41. *Cultural Backlash* by P. Norris, R. Inglehart, P.331; Cambridge University Press, 2019.

reasonable to think (if we follow party lines) that the Democrats being socially liberal would be against slavery while the Republicans being socially conservative would be advocates of slavery. That comparison would be in direct contrast to Lincoln, a Republican, who was against the continued practice of slavery and believed it should be eliminated from our nation entirely.

The polarization of the two political parties was caused by sweeping social trends in our nation that occurred over decades. Norris considers that "the defeat of the Republican mainstream nominees in the 2016 primaries, and Trump's eventual victory, was a culmination of these long-term developments, with his campaign energizing older and non-college-educated white men who felt that their most cherished values and their way of life were being eroded by socially liberal cultural currents."[42]

These are the currents in which the descendants of the Moral Majority are now swimming because of polarization. Much analysis has been done over the most recent presidential elections to determine the amount of influence the evangelical vote has had in determining the outcome of the election. No matter how you analyze the results, there is no doubt that the evangelical vote has been an influential factor. However, the political affiliation of the Religious Right (evangelical leadership) with the Extreme Right has a much broader implication. That implication speaks directly to the power of faith. Faith can be a power to achieve a tremendous amount of good. It can also be a destructive power if applied incorrectly.

THE POWER OF FAITH IN POLITICS

As mentioned previously, I had the opportunity to meet Jerry Falwell Sr. once many years ago. He was visiting our local church, and I was invited back to the pastor's office with a few other lay ministers to meet him. He carried the aura of a rock star as we lined up in a single file to enter the office where we were introduced one at a time. He was a big man, slightly over six feet tall, with a strong grip. He mustered a pleasant smile while

---

42. *Cultural Backlash* by P. Norris, R. Inglehart, P.332; Cambridge University Press, 2019.

greeting us as we shook hands. Each of us was quickly ushered to the side so the next person could get his or her meet and greet. There was no direct conversation. After we all were in place, Falwell said a few words, and then we were ushered out. I later was given a picture of the event, Jerry Falwell and I standing side by side, which I lost many years ago in one of my many moves.

If I were to have a discussion with Pastor Falwell now, I would ask about his time when he started the Moral Majority. I would ask why he started it and what his objectives were although I am pretty sure I know what his answer would be: "to win souls." How do I know that? Because the many times I heard him preach, speak, or teach he would always end up talking about "soul winning." Soul winning is the term used by evangelicals when referring to the process of leading someone to faith in Christ. He was the consummate "evangelical." It was how he built his church, Thomas Roads Baptist Church. He went door-to-door "winning souls" and invited them to church. Then, he taught his church members to do the same.

The point of this trip down memory lane is to explain why I am sure Falwell's motives to align politically with the political powers of the conservative party of our nation were pure. He could never have anticipated the competing forces within the political structure that exist today, forces that confuse the identity of evangelicals because of politics. Russell Moore speaks to that identity:

> If evangelicalism is just political idolatry or populist demagoguery or white nationalism or toxic masculinity or something else, then we can get at the problem merely by addressing all of those. What we must face, though, is the fact that as awful as all those horrors are, they are made worse when they are framed as badges of religious identity. Almost every dictator or demagogue has seen this. With religion, one cannot only claim rapacious power but can do it with the unquestionable authority of the divine. Abuse of power is always horrific; how much

worse, though, when the abuse comes by a weaponized spiritual authority.[43]

When we put our faith in something, we surrender to the authority of the who or what in which we are placing our faith. When we put our faith in God, we are placing our faith in His authority over all things in life and death. That is pretty powerful. Moore is saying when we share our evangelical identity with factions that are contrary to our faith, we empower those factions to do more harm than usual.

How does that happen? There seems to be a transference of faith that occurs by the proximity of competing influences. It is similar to a spiritual misappropriation of faith that transpires by association or observation of repetitious behavior.

Let me give an example. In my early experience of the evangelical church, I was like a sponge soaking up all the details of my newfound faith. I had a favorite teacher and looked forward to his class every week. I was infatuated with his teaching because I found his methods effective and interesting. When it came time for me to begin teaching my own classes, I found myself mimicking my favorite teacher's style of teaching down to the last detail to include pausing between thoughts, licking the corners of my mouth. When I realized what I was doing, I felt embarrassed and quickly abandoned those habits before someone called me on it. In my immaturity of faith and desire to be an impactful teacher, I assumed the delivery was critical. It wasn't until years later that I learned that advances in faith are only attained through investments of faith from one person to another through a spirit of transparency, truthfulness, and integrity. Advances in faith politically cannot be achieved without the same environment.

THE POWER OF MISPLACED FAITH IN POLITICS

The danger of faith in politics is that if it is misguided it often is not obvious until the effect of the misguided faith becomes destructive.

---

43. *Losing Our Religion* by Russell Moore; P. 16; Penguin Random House: Sentinel, 2023.

Faith that is true will never be destructive. Faith in God will always heal, restore, reconcile, and make new. Faith in God will always build up, it will never bring down. When we put our faith in a political leader who has the same faith identity as those in the evangelical faith communities, he or she will never put those following at risk of arrest or imprisonment.

That was not the case surrounding the events prior to the transition of power in the latest presidential election. In a recurring series of events prior to the transition to the newly elected president, thousands of people put their faith in the outgoing president who had been recently defeated in the election. They listened to his direction and acted on his guidance as he assured them he had their best interests at heart. Unfortunately, his motivation was his political survival. He wasn't concerned about the cost his followers would have to pay.

According to an analysis by George Washington University's Program on Extremism, roughly 15 percent of the more than 1,100 people charged for actions on Jan. 6, 2021 were turned in by family members, friends, or acquaintances.[44] In the process, untold relationships have been severed and families have been destroyed.

One such family was the Reffitt family of Plano, Texas. The family of five, including three teenagers ranging in age from fourteen to eighteen, were politically divided. Guy and his wife Nicole were active in the Texas Three Percenters (a far-right anti-government militia). After Trump lost the 2020 election, Guy started talking about going to Washington. Guy recorded himself at the Trump rally on January 6th saying the group's intent was to drag Nancy Pelosi and other lawmakers out of the Capitol building. According to court testimony, Guy helped the mob overrun the police lines using a megaphone to encourage people to break through the barricades.

On January 16, 2021, the FBI raided the Reffitt house and arrested Guy on charges of obstruction of justice and unlawful trespassing related to January 6ᵗ. His teenage son warned the FBI of his father's intent to go to Washington weeks before Guy even left for the rally. Guy was sentenced

---

44. GWU Program on Extremism. Downloaded from https://extremism.gwu.edu/about July 24. 2024.

to 87 months in prison, a sentence he is now serving. Two of the teenagers have left home. Guy's wife moved to the D.C. area after her husband's sentencing to begin holding nightly vigils outside the D.C. jail in support of those she called the "political prisoners" of January 6. One teenager remains in what once was the family residence. This is just one example of a family that was decimated because of actions prompted by a father's misplaced faith in a political leader who only had his own interests in mind at the cost of the future welfare of many families.[45]

These are the times that we live in today. As I write this page, the presidential election process for 2024 is in full swing. The leader of the insurrection of January 6, 2021 is the Republican party's presidential candidate despite that candidate having been indicted on three counts of conspiracy and one count of obstruction regarding the certification of the 2020 election and convicted of 34 felonies for falsifying records to cover up hush money paid to a porn star. Additionally, the candidate received the nomination despite more than 1,100 other citizens of our nation having been charged with criminal activities against our nation for following him.

We must do better than this. We as a people of faith must establish a consistency between our faith and those political leaders we support for our good and the good of our nation. At risk is our democracy as we know it and the future of our faith.

---

45. For more details, see "A family shattered by Jan. 6 tries to forgive and heal" by Dan Rosenzweig-Ziff; Washington Post, Sunday; Sept.10, 2023.

CHAPTER 7

The Land of the
Partially Free

For the first eight years of my education, my parents transported me an hour each way to a private Catholic school in northern New Jersey. Consequently, I looked forward to summer break as an opportunity to spend more time with my local neighborhood friends. A child's time continuum is a little tainted. So much so that when saying goodbye to my school classmates for the summer, we often would say, "See you next year" I can remember believing there was a literal year between school sessions. The summers were so grand and long that it was easy to believe in a kid's mind that we had that much time to enjoy those summer weeks.

Of course, eventually, reality sets into our minds and new perspectives shape our lives. Submitting to the daily grind of career and family, my new focus became my week or weeks-long vacation. I would think about that vacation time all year long, from the minute one ended until the start of the next. What was at first one week, then expanded as time and resources permitted, was the source of great pleasure just thinking how that "downtime" would be spent. Those precious few days each year seemed to be as exhilarating as that summer-long break from school we experienced as children.

Now, having been retired for several years, I can get some clarity as to why those vacations were so meaningful. It was because those breaks from our routines gave us a glimpse of what life would be like if we were free from the encumbrances of work, school, and the demands of the day that were enslaving us at the time. Of course, not literally enslaved, however equally bound in the heart and mind when we covet a freedom of life that we are not able to enjoy. So much so that I can remember becoming depressed on the eve of returning to work, school, or whatever routine was confining me at the time—not clinically depressed, nothing more serious than the sound of an early morning alarm clock couldn't cure. It always amazed me that the act of rising early the next day summoned all purposes of the heart and stamina of the body required to return to the routine until the next break. Thousands of folks repeat that cycle every year.

Being retired affords the opportunity to think about things such as those vacation experiences. It also affords the opportunity to think about what life would be like with no vacations, no breaks, and literally confined to the same routine day in and day out, about what it must have been like to be my grandparents, immigrants from a foreign country not knowing how to read or write in the language of the country in which they suddenly found themselves, or about how it was for my father to be launched into the responsibility of providing for a family of four with an education that halted halfway through the eighth grade and taking on that responsibility after surviving two campaigns of a world war as an Army medic. I remember my father working six or seven days a week in his own business of house painting through most of my youth. Vacations primarily were an occasional Sunday family trip to the Delaware Water Gap for swimming and a picnic.

In all these experiences, no matter how little or how much downtime was available, we all felt completely free to live and enjoy our lives to the fullest extent possible. In my childhood experience, there was never much money, but that did not impede the "pursuit of happiness" as declared in the document that announced our independence to the world in 1776. That is because that pursuit is not relative to money but to our state of peace, safety, and general well-being. Our hearts and minds were not encumbered with fear for the safety of our families. We could live our lives to the fullest extent possible without the worry of the invasion of our privacy or restrictions on our most personal decisions involving the welfare of our relationships.

That, however, has not been the experience for everyone subject to the American experiment throughout its history. That certainly was not the experience of the enslaved people who were at the center of our discussion in the first part of this book. Sadly, that is not the experience of many within the confines of our nation today. Today in our nation, restrictions on our liberties are not based on income, education, or our birthright. They are superimposed on a large segment of our nation's population because of the blending of politics and faith. Similar to the days of Lincoln, the conflation of these two elements has curtailed the freedom of many in our nation.

To grasp the immensity of the scope of the issue we must first come to a common understanding of what the term "freedom for all" means in a nation as large as ours and with our history. As a minimum, "freedom for all" would mean resolving some way to make amends for the generational racial injustices that have been inflicted over time on Black Americans, Jews, Asians, American Indians, and many others. There have not been many efforts dedicated to these issues until the recent discussions on reparations.

LIVING IN SLAVERY'S SHADOW

The 13th Amendment to the Constitution was ratified on December 6, 1865; it banned chattel slavery in the United States. Nonetheless, 100 years later, Black Americans are still living in the shadows of this travesty, constrained from realizing all the liberties offered through their constitutional rights. These fellow citizens, although no longer literally shackled, are still bound in heart, mind, and ways undiscerned by most white Americans and are unable to enjoy complete freedom. In essence, they are a people living in the land of the free with only partial freedom. To them, America is the land of the partially free.

The dehumanizing system of chattel slavery, which considered Black people legal property to be bought, sold, and owned forever. In the history of our nation, many have suffered prejudice and various injustices but none to the extent and severity as the slavery suffered by Black Americans. I cannot imagine the emotional, psychological, and physical impact on the lives of generations of Black Americans as a result of decades of degradation and social inequity. Living in the shadows of slavery, Black Americans were met with a bias and degradation embraced nationwide. Living in those shadows set Black Americans back financially, socially, educationally, and, in a general way, in the American experience. Consequently, the game of life has not been played "on a level playing field" for most Black Americans.

We can understand how difficult it is to compete in anything when circumstances inhibit one person or favor another. Golf uses its handicap system "to level the playing field" between competitors. Our Social Security system provides benefits to a child who loses a parent until they are 18 "to level the playing field" of life somewhat. A widow like my mother can claim her husband's veteran's benefits "to level the playing field" of financial survival after his death.

A similar "level the playing field" concerning the well-being of many California residents has been under debate for years. Recently, California's first-in-the-nation reparations task force released its final report with recommendations for how the state should atone for its history of racial violence and discrimination against Black residents. The document describes detailed examples of "the atrocities committed by Californian state actors who promoted, facilitated, enforced, and permitted the institution of chattel slavery." [46] The effects of these atrocities have persisted for more than a century and have touched nearly all areas of

---

46. "California's first-in-nation reparations task force releases final report" by Abene Clayton, the Guardian, 29 June 2023.

life. The report suggests more than 100 ways to repair the harm, including paying descendants of enslaved people for having suffered under racist actions such as over-policing and housing discrimination. Other cities like Boston and Detroit have established their committees to explore what atoning for injustices suffered by Black Americans could look like.

While "an estimated 80% of Black Californians qualify for reparations under those definitions set by the task force,"[47] many believe the issue is bigger than money. What matters to them is that resources be poured into education or other areas lacking in local Black communities. They want "the playing field to be made level" and the government to acknowledge the wrong that has been done for so many years. And to many others, reparation means simply a recognition of the wrong that was done to them.

The residual impact of slavery in our nation has been implicated in national politics. For example, in the latest Virginia gubernatorial election, the winning candidate talked frequently about race relations and denounced the teaching of critical race theory in Virginia's public school system. More recently, in the present presidential race, the current Governor of Florida (who was seeking the Republican Party nomination) strongly defends de-emphasizing racism in his state's public-school curriculum. He argues that some Black people benefited from being enslaved, and he therefore introduced a new African American history standard, a standard that civil rights leaders and scholars say misrepresents centuries of U.S. reality. The current Vice President of the United States (now the Democratic nominee for president) has openly taken issue with these policies, emphasizing that slavery involved rape, torture, and "some of the worst examples of depriving people of humanity in our world."[48]

Critical race theorists hold the position that racism is inherent in the law and legal institutions of the United States which create and maintain inequalities (social, economic, and political) between whites

47. "The Black church fighting for reparations task force from California" by Scott Wilson, Washington Post, 25 June 2023.

48. "DeSantis doubles down on claim that some benefited from slavery" by Kevin Sullivan and Lori Roza, *Washington Post*, July 23, 2023.

and nonwhites, especially African Americans. I am not a race theorist, but it seems obvious to me that the support of our legal institutions was required to provide a favorable interpretation of the law so that these social, economic, and political inequalities could continue decade after decade for more than a century. I also am not a historian or political analyst, but to imply the atrocities of slavery exacted on thousands is acceptable for the opportunity of some improving their farming or ranching skills is not only a false equivalency, but it also demonstrates a completely amoral character of the person holding that position. That is not someone I want to occupy the most powerful political position in the free world.

The only reason to advance these revised views in educational theory is to resist the increased understanding of slavery's implications for our nation's history. My awakening to these issues began on May 25, 2020. That is the day George Perry Floyd, Jr. was forcibly detained for suspicion of passing a counterfeit $20 bill. Police officer Derek Chauvin knelt on Mr. Floyd's neck and back for nine minutes and 29 seconds. Floyd's dying words, "I can't breathe," became a rallying cry after his murder as protests against police brutality, especially toward Black people, quickly spread around the globe.[49] The events of that day and the following months affected me as it did millions globally. I finally "saw" the racial plight of Black people that has been ongoing since the inception of our nation. The dramatic indifference to this man's life pouring out of him under the knee of a police officer dramatically affected the world, but only for a short while. It wasn't long until the outrage was gone, and things returned to as they were without any lasting change to national behaviors, until the effort for reparations took hold.

So, where are the faith communities of our nation in this fight for reparations? Reverend Amos C. Brown has pastored the Third Baptist Church in San Francisco since 1976. He has been a powerful voice for reparations in his pulpit and for the California Commission on Reparations. The Black church was an engine for civil rights advocacy in California and other parts of the nation from the 1950s through the

---

49. As described in Wikipedia under "George Perry Floyd, Jr."

1970s. However, some African American scholars characterize the Black church's role in reparations as marginal. James Lance Taylor, a political science professor at the University of San Francisco and a member of the city's reparations task force states, "This [reparations] has been a blind spot in the Black church. The Black church here is not dead. But it [the Black church] is exhausted, and we're hoping the reparations movement will wake them back up to the social issues surrounding them."[50]

This is the heritage of slavery in our nation. The result is a large portion of our nation's Black community living in the shadow of slavery and they are looking for a "leveling of the playing field." This is not a cause for only Black Americans or the Black Church. It is a cause for all in our nation and all communities of faith.

GIVE ME YOUR TIRED AND POOR

"Give me your tired, your poor, your huddled masses yearning to breathe free" is the famous inscription on the Statue of Liberty located on Liberty Island in New York Harbor in New York City. It gives me great comfort to think my grandfather with his parents and siblings saw that same statue when they immigrated from Italy. It is a clear message standing in the waters outside of one of our great cities, announcing to immigrants such as my family that they are welcome and that they are welcome with open arms. I am quite certain many immigrants in our nation today do not feel that way. These are different times with different circumstances.

Immigration is often characterized as a "political football." That metaphor applies to this and many other issues that receive attention during the political campaign season but little attention to fixing the situation after the election. Immigration is kicked back and forth between the two political parties, each blaming the other for not solving the problem. The truth of the matter is we have gone through countless administrations and sessions of Congress with each political party in

---

50. "The Black church fighting for reparations task force from California" by Scott Wilson, *Washington Post*, 25 June 2023.

control at various times with little progress being made on the immigration dilemma our nation faces today. In the last three administrations, we have gone from Obama, the "Deporter in Chief" and the protector of the "Dreamers," to Trump's building the wall at Mexico's expense, to Biden being accused of doing nothing to help but only making the situation worse. Currently, Congress ignores finding a solution while governors in red states rent buses and deposit thousands of illegal immigrants in the cities of blue states. This point was recently dramatically illustrated when the Senate passed a bi-partisan immigration bill proposing funding and administrative fixes needed to improve the immigration crisis at our borders. The measure was turned down for consideration in the House of Representatives because it would appear as a political win for the current administration leading up to an election year. Once again, politics was more important than bipartisanship.

Figures recently quoted on CNN[51] described the immigration issue as growing worse by the day. The following are some of the quoted figures: 3.8 million migrant encounters on the Southwest border over the last two years; 140,000 Border Patrol apprehensions on the US-Mexico border's first 20 days of September 2023; 2.2 million total apprehensions achieved through September 2023 meet the total apprehensions experienced throughout all of 2022.

The reality of the problem is that immigration is a worldwide dilemma. The political upheaval throughout the world has produced unprecedented numbers of people searching for political asylum. Add to those numbers the people running from the destruction of war, like the one in Ukraine, and we have a flood of immigrants affecting not only our nation but also many other nations of the world. They all are looking for what we have: those "certain inalienable rights that have been endowed by our Creator" which include such things as "life, liberty, and the pursuit of happiness," which our Declaration of Independence states as true for our nation and the Constitution promises to deliver to us.

---

51. CNN (Cable News Network) show, "Smerconish" (Michael Smerconish); Sept.29, 2023.

Many are attracted to our nation because it is the land that offers freedom to all. But many who live here are only at best partially free. I have ministered to many families from Central and South America, including some that are here illegally. They are welcomed in our churches; their immigration status is never an issue. I have taught the children of migrant workers in our public schools not knowing if they were legal residents or not. I have taught students who were exceptionally bright and serious students who were suddenly gone from school because of their migrant family status.

These examples represent people who are here among us, living in the shadows, unable to enjoy the complete concept of living free because the Constitution does not apply to them. They no doubt are enjoying relief from whatever conditions prompted them to come to our nation. Why else would they stay in a country that makes it clear they are not wanted, at least by most Americans? But they are wanted by those American employers who need them to continue to do the work they do for the wage they pay which Americans will not do. They willingly do the work for the opportunity to embrace whatever portion of the freedom of life that they can while they are here.

This limited liberty being offered to these people is the type of liberty that enslaves, which is not liberty at all. Yes, they have freedom, but they live a life of curtailed rights and submission to an authority whose actions are often not clearly understood. How does one explain being bused from Texas to New York City and being released on the streets of the city? The answer is one can't explain actions like these legitimately. They are political gimmicks that try to pass blame from one elected official to another. These immigrants are tricked, persuaded, or, in some cases, lied to about a job waiting for them in the new location. We owe it to them and to ourselves to fix this problem with compassion and with urgency. It is our legacy as a nation. Immigration is in our nation's DNA.

If one listens to the political rhetoric occurring during the current election cycle, two prevailing arguments describe the reason for the current dilemma. The first, mentioned previously, is Biden's fault, and the second is the demand for the latest illegal drug of choice, fentanyl.

The first is simply not true. The second has some relevance, but that is a separate and distinct issue being addressed by the current administration.

Law enforcement agencies have so far seized over 55 million pills of fentanyl this year and more than 9,000 pounds of powder containing the deadly drug. The Drug Enforcement Administration is on pace to seize more fentanyl in 2023 than in any previous year, a yield that continues to grow annually.[52]

China is the key source of precursor chemicals which are often shipped to Mexico and used by cartels to produce fentanyl which is then brought over the border.[53] If you take the time to check several news sources, you will hear the current Secretary of State challenging China's involvement in the fentanyl problem as an example of this being an international issue.

Drug experts point to U.S. consumers hooked on opioids as the driver of the fentanyl market. While some of the same cartels pushing fentanyl into the country also smuggle people, they do so through different pathways. The drug and the chemicals used for the processing of the drug are more likely to enter through ports of entry. Migrants typically enter through the porous points between the points of entry.[54]

I am particularly sensitive to this felonious political argument concerning our nation's drug problem today. I was fortunate enough to be part of the Department of Defense team designated to support President George Bush's "war on drugs" in September 1989. I had the privilege of working with the President's Office of National Drug Control Policy (ONDCP) in leveraging DOD technologies to curtail the flow of illegal drugs into our nation at that time. I was part of the Drug Enforcement Agency's covert operation along the Mexican border that discovered the first of many drug smuggling tunnels. It was a successful mission, using both DOD technologies and personnel working under the operational

---

52. "DEA has seized over 55 million fentanyl pills in 2023 so far, Garland says" by Robert Legare: Sept.26, 2023, CBS News.

53. "Blinken under pressure to push China on role in lethal fentanyl trade when he visits Beijing" by Kylie Atwood & Jennifer Hansler, Feb. 2, 2023, CNN.

54. "Is America's immigration crisis causing the fentanyl epidemic?" by Anna Giaritelli, July 13, 2022, *Washington Examiner*.

control of the DEA agents on the scene. That was just one dimension of a complex problem then as it is now.

The most formidable task faced in the 1990s was the overwhelming number of shipping containers entering the ports of entry, many containing drugs. There were many proposed methods to try to inspect as many of these containers as possible, but the numbers were too great to inspect every container. If you drive by any port of entry today, you will see hundreds of these huge containers stacked high as far as you can see.

These difficult and complex issues were being faced then as they are today. I do not remember in those days any political criticism of the administration's attempts to solve this very difficult threat to our nation. Maybe I was too busy to hear it or just not interested in listening. However, I do think the political climate differed. Politics has always been politics, but now it seems to be untethered from any sense of national priorities and has given way to pure preferences.

We must expect our elected officials to quit using immigration as a political football and work toward a solution to this complex problem. Governors need to work together instead of targeting each other. Congressmen need to work across the aisle with the current administration to solve the problem. We as a nation must unite and not accept any less from our elected officials. It would be a great pleasure to hear our elected officials across party lines working together to solve the common problem of immigration.

ARMED TO KILL

As a boy, I enjoyed watching the adventures of the Wild, Wild West many evenings on television with my family. My favorite was "The Rifleman," starring Chuck Conners as rancher Lucas McCain, who lived in the fictional town of North Fork with his son Mark, played by Jonny Crawford. I was always sure to be seated, ready to watch, at the beginning of each show because the opening scene showed Lucas firing his Winchester Model 1892 rifle. That specific rifle was customized to allow repeated firing by cycling its lever action as well as a second modification that allowed the rifle to be fired with one hand using a technique known as "spin-cocking."[55] It was a thing of beauty to watch as I sat mesmerized by the sheer power of bullets flying at the bad guys with such ease.

However, it became apparent to me that my love affair with guns was not going to carry over into adulthood when in college I was required to fire an M1 Rifle and a 45-caliber pistol on the range as part of my Reserve Officer Training Corps (ROTC) requirements. Difficult weapons to handle, they were extremely loud, and I often missed the target completely. In those days protection for ears was limited to whatever was available to stuff into them. Consequently, it was quite common for ears to be ringing several hours after firing on the range. It was such an unpleasant experience I have never shot a weapon since and have no desire to do so now many years later.

My intense dislike for guns has only been magnified in my heart and mind over the years because of the rampant gun violence in our nation. I have come to realize that my animus toward guns is rooted in two experiences, one being at the ROTC gun range. The other occurred when I was very young, probably no more than six or seven years old. We were visiting my cousin when he decided to show my older brother his Dad's German luger brought back from World War II in Europe. As my brother was admiring it, the gun misfired with a loud blast followed by a stream of adults screaming while running up the stairs. Fortunately, the bullet lodged in the corner of the ceiling, and no one was hurt.

It occurs to me now that a frightening early childhood experience, which could have been fatal to any of us kids at the time, never came to mind the many times I watched "The Rifleman" or any other program with gun violence. Yet, the one experience on the rifle range, several years later, convinced me that I never wanted to shoot a gun again. Why is that? Well, I was seduced by the "commercialized" version of gun violence. The commercialized version suppresses the debilitating noise and avoids showing the violent destruction caused by the weapon when aimed at someone or something. I have to believe that the one experience on the

---

55. As described in Wikipedia under "The Rifleman"

rifle range touched that childhood fear from many years before once the noise was unabated and not cosmetically packaged. Witnessing the dirt flying from missed shots at the target and seeing the destruction caused to the target when hit reminded me that bullet that tore a hole in the ceiling could have ripped through any one of us.

More important, I believe the same is happening today on a much larger scale. I believe our nation has been seduced by the "commercialization" of gun violence by Hollywood, the video gaming industry, the gun industry, and the political lobby that has paralyzed Congress and persuaded faith communities to be apathetic toward the rampant gun violence in our nation today. The result is a large portion of our nation today being robbed of their Constitutional liberties of domestic tranquility, domestic defense, and general welfare, worrying if their children will return home safely from school, college, a concert, a mall, or a church service. Many are living a life in fear of gun violence. The liberty of some is enslaving the lives of others because of guns. We are a nation armed to kill.

Without question, the use of automatic weapons and the expanded cartridge capabilities of other guns offer the biggest threat to our nation when it involves gun violence. *The Washington Post* staff spent seven months examining the AR-15's role in America's gun violence dilemma. They interviewed more than 200 people, including firearms industry executives and lobbyists, gun owners, shooting survivors and victims' families, lawmakers, trauma surgeons, first responders, activists, armed militants, academics, and ballistic experts. They also reviewed more than 1,000 pages of documents, including internal company records, court and regulatory filings, and autopsy reports. The *Post* partnered with Ipsos (a global market research firm) to survey hundreds of AR-15 owners.[56] The following are some of their findings:

- The AR-15's rise over the past two decades was sparked by a dramatic reversal in strategy by the country's biggest gun

---

56. "We spent 7 months examining the AR-15's role in America. Here's what we learned." By *The Washington Post* Staff; March 27, 2023.

companies to invest in a product that many in the industry had long viewed as anathema to their culture and traditions.

- While handguns account for the most gun-related killings in the United States, sales of AR-15s surge in times of tragedy and political change.

- About 1 in 20 U.S. adults (about 16 million) own at least one AR-15, with self-defense the most popular reason for owning one.

- The AR-15s are lethal and destructive, allowing shooters to fire in rapid succession high-velocity bullets that create a blast effect when penetrating a body that blows up organs and pulverizes bones.

- In response to right-wing violence and intimidation linked to the AR-15, some far-left activists have begun to form armed groups, often turning to AR-15 as their weapon.

- Police departments have started equipping officers with AR-15s (once limited to SWAT Teams only) because patrolled neighborhoods are flooded with AR-15s.

- Many gun violence experts and law enforcement veterans say that restricting the sizes of ammunition magazines would lessen the carnage caused by AR-15s and other guns.

Let me summarize the preceding findings in a few thoughts. A revised business strategy has produced a lethal gun which is the preferred method of defense for approximately 16 million people. This lethal gun is the weapon of choice for both left and right extremists. Additionally, this lethal weapon has become a standard issue for police to adequately protect their local communities. We are a nation that is armed to kill in the most violent way as a means of defense against aggression from extremists and protection of the innocent, all the while ignoring the simplest way to reduce carnage by simply limiting the sizes of ammunition magazines for these weapons.

Our nation is enslaved by the prevailing gun violence that is permitted to exist because of political preferences that many justify as perceived

Constitutional rights. I do not understand how anyone can think the founding fathers of our nation intended for the American people to be subjected to this type of violence when they penned our Constitution and its supporting amendments. A read of the Constitution's opening paragraph clearly illustrates that the authors desired a different outcome. It reads as follows.

> *"We the people of the United States, in order to form a more perfect union, establish justice, insure domestic tranquility, provide for a common defense, promote the general welfare, and secure the blessings of Liberty to ourselves, and our posterity, do ordain and establish this Constitution for the United States of America."*

Our founding fathers desired the people of this nation to live a life of liberty where homes were tranquil (peaceful), where people felt safe, and where the laws of the land were for the benefit of the general welfare of all people. This was the desire for themselves, their families, and for us as well (their posterity). I contend that none of those elements (peace, safety, security) exist in the homes and the lives of the people in our nation who have been subject to these mass shootings in our churches, schools, and streets. Second Amendment advocates ignore the context of the amendment being written in terms of a militia because there were no state or local police, no State National Guards, nor any Department of Defense. In fact, those who constructed the Bill of Rights were against militarized homes as indicated by the Third Amendment forbidding any soldier from being quartered in a private residence. I am sure the founding fathers never envisioned the possibility of an individual resident having the equivalent firepower of the Continental Army in their home as we currently have in some cases.

So, where are the faith communities in this current gun dilemma? I find them strangely silent. I find many faith communities very vocal in their defense of life for the unborn. I do not criticize that; I have done the same for many years and will discuss this topic at length next in this chapter. But where are the faith communities in defense of the children being slaughtered while attending school, church, or at the mall? It is time for all communities of faith to cry out in equal defense of the born when it comes to this onslaught of guns in our nation.

THE FREEDOM TO CHOOSE

At the heart of the concept of our nation is freedom, liberty, and the ability to exercise our choice of religion or not. To integrate a preferred religious view into the legislative process of our nation flies in the face of the founding father's vision of separation of church and state. The purpose of that separation is to ensure that a state-preferred religion is not incorporated into the governance of our nation. What we are experiencing in our nation today is exactly such an incorporation in disguise. Through the politicization of faith and the polarization of evangelical Christians, our legislative process is being influenced state by state, and more broadly at the federal level, to redefine reproductive rights in our nation. The freedom to choose in this area of our lives is subtly, deliberately being controlled with the eventual goal of eliminating that liberty from our nation.

On Friday, June 24, 2022, the US Supreme Court overturned Roe v. Wade, the landmark piece of legislation that made access to abortion a federal right in the United States. The decision dismantled 50 years of reproductive liberty in our nation and paved the way for individual states to curtail or outright ban abortion rights. Because of trigger laws put in place before the ruling, abortion was outlawed in many states automatically or through state action following the decision. In addition, at the time of the ruling, Justice Clarence Thomas wrote that certain other landmark rulings should be reconsidered, including established rights to contraception access, same-sex relationships, and same-sex marriage.[57] Justice Thomas' remarks should have been construed as a warning that further assaults on established liberties would follow. Since that time

---

57. *Roe v Wade Overturned: What it Means, What's Next* by Patty Housman; June 29, 2022. Downloaded from American University College of Arts & Sciences News, https:// www.american.edu/cas/news/roe-v-wade-overturned-what-it-means-whats-next.cfm.

there have been bills introduced in both houses of Congress proposing a national abortion ban.[58]

Justice Samuel Alito wrote the court majority decision overturning Roe stating that the 1973 ruling, which had been upheld by repeated subsequent high court decisions for 50 years in our nation, "must be overruled" because they were "egregiously wrong," the arguments "exceptionally weak" and so "damaging" they amounted to "an abuse of judicial authority." The other justices voted according to their political dispositions. Justices Thomas, Gorsuch, Kavanaugh, Barrett, and Roberts, all appointed by Republican Presidents, joined the Alito opinion. Justice Roberts concurred in judgment only, stating he would have limited the decision to the case in front of the court only and not made the decision a unilateral reversal of Roe, calling the decision "a serious jolt to the legal system." Justices Breyer, Sotomayor, and Kagan, having all been appointed by Democratic presidents, dissented from Alito's opinion.[59]

The abortion landscape in our nation has been in a state of flux since the Supreme Court decision. The latest overview shows:

- Abortion is currently illegal or heavily restricted in at least 16 states; that includes. states with near-total bans on abortion as well as those with bans at roughly six weeks gestational age or after the detection of fetal cardiac activity.

- At least six other states have laws in place that pave the way to ban or severely restrict access to abortion.

- Some state laws restricting abortion are currently blocked by courts while legal challenges make their way through the courts.

- Some states have older laws on the books that leave the current legal status of abortion unclear.

---

58. *What You Need to Know about the Bill to Ban Abortion Nationwide* by Maggie Jo Buchanan; Sep.16, 2022. Downloaded from Center for American Progress, https://www.americanprogress.org/article/what-you-need-to-know-about-the-bill-to-ban-abortion-nationwide/.

59. "Supreme Court overturns Roe v. Wade, ending right to abortion upheld for decades" by Nina Totenberg, Sarah McCammon, *All Things Considered* (NPR), updated June 24, 2022.

- Several additional states have pre-viability gestational age restrictions, ranging from 12 to 22 weeks. [60]

We are a divided nation when it comes to reproductive rights since the overturning of Roe. As of now, approximately 57% of our nation has had no restrictive measures introduced to their liberty or social rights while approximately 43% have had some severe restrictions imposed on those liberties. Those numbers are certain to change as impending court decisions are finalized with the possibility of half of our nation facing severely restricted reproductive liberties. That would be fine if everyone within those restricted locations had the same political persuasion, faith, or social needs. The fact is that some of those states that now have the most restrictive rights represent some of the poorest areas in our nation with the greatest social needs.

As of this writing about 3/4 of white evangelical Protestants (74%) think abortion should be illegal in all or most cases. By contrast, 84% of religiously unaffiliated Americans say abortion should be legal in all or most cases, as do 66% of Black protestants, 60% of white Protestants who are not evangelical, and 56% of Catholics.[61]

The polarization of reproductive rights within faith communities began almost 50 years ago. Evangelical publications in the 1960s indicate that the prevailing notion before Roe v Wade (decided in 1973) was that abortion was not a desirable outcome but was not considered an unqualified evil as it is today by many evangelicals. In a 1971 resolution, the Southern Baptist Convention encouraged "legislation that will allow the possibility of abortion under such conditions as rape, incest, clear evidence of severe fetal deformity, and carefully ascertained evidence of the likelihood of damage to the emotional, mental, and physical health of

---

60. "Here's where abortions are now banned or severely restricted" By Haidee Chu, Wynne Davis, Katie Daugert, Kristin Gourlay, Sarah Knight, Carmel Wroth, *Reproductive Rights in America* (NPR), updated Sept. 20, 2023.

61. "Public Opinion on Abortion;" Pew Research Center; fact Sheet on Views on Abortion 1995-2022, May 17, 2022.

the mother." That same resolution was affirmed in both 1974 and 1976, as well."[62]

So, what changed the views of evangelicals? Many leaders of the Religious Right in the 1980s and 1990s viewed abortion as an activating issue to encourage church members to oppose abortion through their political support. "They knew that the millions of evangelicals who for decades had been tepid about political engagement would have a hard time ignoring graphic images of aborted fetuses."[63]

They were exactly right. How do I know that? As mentioned before I was in the heart of the Religious Right fervor during the 1980s and early 1990s. Deeply involved in Jerry Falwell ministries, I marched with groups carrying those pictures, and I voted in every presidential election with one criterion in mind: support Republican candidates for national office because they were the "right to life" party. Nothing else mattered. I have great remorse over those days for being as politically manipulated as I was. I have written extensively about my faith journey away from that bondage.[64]

I call that time my faith journey bondage because my view was restricted to my doctrine of faith at the time and rejected other faith considerations as valid. I did not attempt to understand the reproductive rights of women. I did not attempt to try to understand the social needs of women and families who do not have health care or the means to attain it. Last, I did not consider that for many people their reproductive rights have nothing to do with their faith.

It was only after realizing the hypocrisy in my life concerning abortion that my views changed. Long before my faith was an active part of my life, I was nearly complicit in the financing of an abortion—saved from complicity only because the woman turned out not to be pregnant. Otherwise, I would have freely participated in the termination of the unwanted pregnancy. It was at that moment I realized there are probably

62. *20 Myths about Religion and Politics in America* by Ryan P. Burge; P. 122; Fortress Press, 2022.

63. Ibid, P.123

64. *The Evidence of Things Unseen* by Jerry Aveta; P.109-111; West Bow Press, 2021.

many men like me. Men who many years ago were willing to participate in an abortion, and perhaps did, but now we piously stand against it while we silently watch women fight for their reproductive rights, in essence, rights over their bodies.

FINAL THOUGHTS ON LIBERTY FOR SOME

History tells us that many years ago our nation faced similar circumstances. Then the issue was slavery. Similarly, the nation was politically polarized. People of the same faith then were on opposite sides of the issue.

An early chapter described a newly elected President Lincoln searching for some way to begin closing the divide that existed in our nation at that time. Briefly recapturing the situation, President Lincoln believed the nation lived under a constitution framed with the intention of preventing the spread of slavery to allow the nation to grow in its experience and eventually eliminate slavery from the land. Lincoln stated,

> I do not mean to say we are bound to follow implicitly in whatever our fathers did. To do so, would be to discard all the lights of current experience—to reject all progress— all improvement. What I do say is, that if we would supplant the opinions and policy of our fathers in any case, we should do so upon evidence so conclusive, and argument so clear, that even their great authority, fairly considered and weighed, cannot stand.[65]

I see no such similar reasoning being considered in the political landscape of our nation today. There is no consideration of constitutional intent, lessons learned from experience, or anything else. It seems the vast majority of policies, legislative considerations, and general guidance from our elected officials most of the time is delivered with a polarized bias in order for that party to maintain control of our nation. Objective analysis no longer exists. Such is an environment that fosters freedom for some, not liberty for all.

---

65. *And There Was Light* by Jon Meacham, P.182; Random House, 2022.

CHAPTER 8

Liberty Under Seige

From 2014 to 2016, the Ebola outbreak killed more than 11,000 people in West Africa. President Obama at the time was very deliberate in taking several precautionary measures to mitigate any effect of the outbreak if it reached our area of the world. Two of his most significant actions were to establish a response coordinator within his administration in the event of an incident and to produce a 69-page document titled "Playbook for Early Response to High-Consequence Emerging Infectious Disease Threats and Biological Incidents."[66] I was a big Obama fan, but I remember thinking at that time that this response was a little too much. I believed the chances of a deadly pandemic reaching our shores from the other side of the world were highly unlikely. I did not believe something that deadly could migrate all the way across the thousands of miles of ocean and have much of an effect on our nation. Four years later in 2020, I quickly realized how foolish my previous thinking had been as I watched COVID-19 spread throughout our nation. When the pandemic reached

---

66. *"How US Presidents Have Handled Public Health Crisis* by Patsy Widakuswara; www.voanews.com; March 30, 2020.

Indianapolis, Indiana, the matriarch of my family, my 90-year-old aunt, was lost. I then became a believer in the lethality of a pandemic. Countless lives were lost with that same misconception that I previously had: it will never happen here.

Similarly, I have spent a large portion of my adult years under the misconception that our nation could never experience another Civil War. I could not imagine an issue as divisive as slavery ever consuming our nation again. I believed that our nation had matured and would never allow something that destructive to our liberty ever to reoccur. Similar to my lack of understanding of how pandemics spread, I had no understanding of how the next assault on our nation's liberties would occur. On January 6, 2021, I again realized how foolish my thinking was about civil war violence never occurring again in our nation. Once again I became a believer in what I thought was impossible being possible as I watched the insurrection on our Capitol just a few miles from my residence.

Unlike the days of Lincoln, the threat to our liberties today is not the result of one divisive issue but several. While any one of these current issues taken alone is not capable of severing our nation, the confluence of the multitude of issues has seemingly brought our nation to a similar place of divide as was in the days of Lincoln. Let me refer to this year's American Values Survey conducted by the Public Religion Research Institute (PRRI) with the Brookings Institution to clarify this point.

This year's PRRI survey describes the American people as very conflicted and increasingly not possessing a shared set of beliefs or values across a wide range of political issues. Key findings showed a growing amount of support for political violence, a willingness to ignore the rule of law to win political power, and a belief in untrue conspiracy theories. Antidemocratic convictions were found more acute among white evangelical Protestants who yearn for a return to "traditional American values" in a country they believe "is moving in the wrong direction."[67]

---

67. "Apocalypticism": Polling expert reveals the root of "panic among conservative White Christians"; *Salon*; by Chauncey DeVega; 6 November 2023.

I do not have the knowledge or experience to explain how our country arrived in the state described by the PRRI survey. But Steven Levitsky and Daniel Ziblatt, professors of government at Harvard University, have documented that experience in *Tyranny of the Minority*.[68] I am summarizing their key points here but recommend their book for a detailed account of our nation's course of events leading up to the present condition.

DEMOCRACY ABANDONED (DESCRIBED BY THREE EVENTS)

Like explorers fixating on known celestial bodies to determine their position on Earth, Levitsky and Ziblatt align three social-political events in our nation's history that give us a clear fixation on the state of democracy in our nation today. These three events span more than 100 years, stretching from sometime during the Civil War to as late as a few years ago.

FIRST EVENT

The Reconstruction Era began near the end of the Civil War and ended more than a decade later. The main goals were to rebuild the nation, integrate the former Confederate states into the union, and address the social, political, and economic impacts of slavery. During this period, the 13th, 14th, and 15th Amendments were added to the Constitution. These amendments respectively abolished slavery, established the rights of all persons born or naturalized in the United States to be citizens, and established the right to vote regardless of race, color, or previous condition of servitude. However, Reconstruction had significant shortcomings. Black people were subject to Klan violence, starvation, disease, death, and brutal treatment by Union soldiers. Congress federalized the protection of civil rights in response to violent attacks against Black people in the

---

68. *Tyranny of the Minority* by Steven Levitsky and Daniel Ziblatt; P.92; Crown Publishing, 2023.

South, and ex-Confederate states were required to guarantee freedmen's civil rights before rejoining the Union.[69]

SECOND EVENT

Almost 100 years after the end of the Reconstruction era, President Lyndon Johnson's address to a joint session of Congress in November 1963 declared the following: "We have talked long enough in this country about equal rights. We have talked for one hundred years or more. It is time now to write the next chapter, and to write it in the books of law." With that proclamation, what followed was a series of court decisions and reforms that culminated in the Civil Rights Act (1964) and the Voting Rights Act (1965) establishing a solid legal foundation for multiracial democracy.[70]

The Civil Rights Act of 1964 outlawed discrimination based on race, color, religion, sex, and national origin. In addition, it prohibited unequal application of voter registration requirements, racial segregation in schools and public accommodations, and employment discrimination. The Voting Rights Act of 1965 prohibited racial discrimination in voting. The act sought to secure the right to vote for racial minorities throughout the country, especially in the South.[71]

It must be noted that during the 100 years that passed between the end of the Civil War and the Civil Rights Act of 1964, there had been other civil rights initiatives. The Civil Rights Act of 1875 was limited by the Supreme Court decision ruling that Congress did not have the power to prohibit discrimination in the private sector. The Civil Rights Act of 1957 signed by President Dwight D. Eisenhower increased the protection of African American voting rights.

It is important to pause at this point and note the obvious. After the conclusion of a devasting war over civil rights that pitted Americans

69. Wikipedia, The Free Encyclopedia; "Reconstruction era"
70. *Tyranny of the Minority* by Steven Levitsky and Daniel Ziblatt; P.92; Crown Publishing, 2023.
71. Wikipedia The Free Encyclopedia; "Civil Rights Act of 1965", "Voting Rights Act of 1965".

against one another, resulting in an untold amount of destruction and more than 600,000 deaths, it is apparent that as a nation we were not ready to reconcile our differences. For the next 100 years Americans would continue not only to ignore the civil rights of Black Americans but also to continue enacting physical, emotional, and spiritual abuse on people subjected to the atrocities of slavery. Physical abuse took the shape of working long hours harvesting crops in very difficult conditions with few tools or accommodations. Emotional abuse occurred through the separation or destruction of the individual Black family units. Spiritual abuse resulted from the dehumanizing treatment of being bought, sold, and treated like livestock. Slavery was distinctive in its abuse, being savage enough to attack the mind, soul, and body all at the same time. In so doing, it could be considered a grave moral issue that persisted in our nation.

It was our elected leaders, on both sides of the political aisle, who had the courage to act against these continued moral violations, to attempt to put an end to Americans abusing other Americans. The reforms specified in the Civil Rights Acts of the 1960s were backed by a majority of both parties. At the time, there was a Jim Crow faction in the Democratic Party that vehemently opposed civil rights. These bills could not have passed without strong Republican support. In the end, more than 80 percent of House and Senate Republicans supported these bills while Democrat support was 61 percent in the House and 69 percent in the Senate.[72] (Note: Jim Crow laws introduced in the Southern United States in the late 19th and early 20th centuries enforced racial segregation, "Jim Crow" being a pejorative term for African Americans.[73])

On June 25, 2013, the Supreme Court struck down a key provision of the Voting Rights Act of 1965. The ruling held that the formula used to determine which jurisdictions needed federal oversight when changing their voting laws was outdated and unconstitutional. The

72. *Tyranny of the Minority* by Steven Levitsky and Daniel Ziblatt P.93; Crown Publishing, 2023.
73. Wikipedia The Free Encyclopedia; "Jim Crow Laws".

ruling gutted the Voting Rights Act by eliminating critical protections from discrimination.[74]

THIRD EVENT

In August 2021 legislation passed the House of Representatives restoring the critical provision struck down by the Supreme Court eight years prior. That legislation was rejected by the Senate and no other legislation has been proposed since. What follows is Levitsky and Ziblatt's description of the current state of our union approximately 60 years after the historic Civil Rights Acts of the 1960s.

Sixty years later, that Republican Party has become unrecognizable. The same party that was pivotal in passing the Voting Rights Act of 1965 was unanimous in rejecting federal legislation to restore it in 2021. But the Republican Party has done more than walk away from voting rights. It has, in the words of the sober-minded British publication *The Economist*, "walked away from democracy."[75]

In other words, Levitsky and Ziblatt are implying that one of the two major political parties in our nation has *abandoned democracy*.

I am not a politician, a student of government, or a Harvard professor, so let me describe what I think Levitsky and Ziblatt are saying in simple layman's terms. At the heart of our democracy is the ability as a citizen to elect our governing officials in a fair and direct manner. That is probably the most important liberty afforded to us among the many other freedoms we enjoy in our democracy. Any attempt to tamper with that freedom either through artificial tests on qualifications to vote or encumbrances put in place to make voting more difficult is an attack on our liberty and is an existential threat to our democracy. To deny a critical piece of the Civil Rights Voting Act without any remedial action for ten years or more is, according to Levitsky and Ziblatt, the equivalency of walking away from the governing responsibilities of our elected officials

---

74. www.brennancenter.org/our-work/court-cases/shelby-county-v-holder

75. "Tyranny of the Minority" by Steven Levitsky and Daniel Ziblatt; P.93; Crown Publishing, 2023.

and thereby rendering our democracy inactive and/or ineffective. This appears to be the strategy of one of the two political parties in our nation today. Levitsky and Ziblatt describe this strategy as a choice of *racial conservatism over civil rights*.

RACIAL CONSERVATISM

In my experience, *racial conservatism* is a term that is not used in the mainstream media. A quick search on some conservative websites yielded the following definition:

> *Racial conservatism* means a recognition of certain truths about race, and the commitment to preserving a particular race, namely the white race, and a society and civilization in which its characteristics, qualities, and talents will be the norm and can evolve and develop themselves without impossible hindrance, unlike in liberal society.[76]

Once again, let us pause to discuss the obvious. The *Merriam-Webster Dictionary* definition of racism is as follows: "A belief that race is a fundamental determinant of human traits and capacities and that racial differences produce an inherent superiority of a particular race." Compare this to the intent of "racial conservatism" which is to "commit to the preservation of the white race as the norm to be developed without hindrance," which implies that the white race has an inherent superiority and/or priority compared to the other races of color. I would characterize "racial conservatism" as a form of racism because there is an implicit judgment that other races are inferior to the white race. It remains a silent judgment, never publicly verbalized except in political code words referred to as "dog whistles." This is where the unseen interacts with the seen, in other words, the natural with the supernatural. I characterize it as similar to the "spirit of slavery" that influenced all people of our nation, sacred and secular alike. The difference is that slavery bound one race in

---

76. View from the Right; www.amnation.com; "Racial Conservatism"; June 2012.

chains, while "racial conservatism" is trying to enslave non-white races through a political disadvantage in exercising their constitutional rights. Levitsky and Ziblatt use the term "racial conservatism" to describe the strategic decision of the Republican party to win the support of the white electorate in the South. Let's look at how that strategy evolved over time from the Civil War until today.

THE EVOLUTION OF CIVIL RIGHTS

Growing up in the north I was oblivious to any of the social-political dynamics of the South. My first exposure to the South came as a young teen when I accompanied my parents to Lexington, Virginia where my brother was attending college. I remember looking at the rolling hills of the Shenandoah Valley while heading south on Virginia Highway Route 11. With the Blue Ridge Mountains in plain sight, we passed numbers of small mom-and-pop shops selling all kinds of Civil War souvenirs. At my brother's college, I observed a life-size statue of "Stonewall" Jackson who was a general officer in the Confederate Army and a teacher at that college before the Civil War. Also, there were several graves of students who were drafted into the Civil War while attending college there and died during the Battle of New Market nearby. It was my first exposure to the war between the states outside of a classroom textbook or a TV production. I then realized the Civil War left a meaningful, visible impression on the South even after these many years.

Putting aside the horrific loss of life on both sides of the Civil War, the South obviously suffered the greater consequence simply because the majority of the fighting occurred on Southern soil. Perhaps the greatest consequences to the South were first, the major change to the agricultural business model with the loss of slave labor and second, the radical change in social structure elevating a class of people formerly regarded as slaves to an equal status of citizen. It is no wonder that the acceptance of all the proposed social reforms was slow to be accepted in the South. Consequently, the resistance to change left the South a highly contested political target that resulted in swings in political preferences by the people in the South throughout the years.

From 1890 to 1930, the GOP controlled the presidency for 30 of 40 years and the Senate for 32 of those years. During those years of GOP dominance, the predominately Democratic South was of no critical interest to the Republican party. The GOP was successful with little political support from the South because then it was a party quite different from the one you see today. The bulk of GOP support came from factions that included northeastern manufacturing interests, midwestern farmers, small-town conservatives, and white protestant voters outside the South. That was the "conservatism" that was offered then by the GOP, quite different from that offered today.[77]

However, the Great Depression that occurred throughout the 1920s and the resultant political initiatives known as the New Deal began to change the political posture of our nation. Introduced by President Franklin D. Roosevelt in 1933, the New Deal involved a massive works program and the availability of loans to help recover the economy of the nation. Consequently, millions of urban Black and white working-class voters rejected the Republicans, and the New Deal Democrats became the new majority party. The Democrats won five consecutive presidential elections between 1932 and 1948.

But once again the political tides of the nation began to change, starting late in the 1930s. At that time, the Democratic Party forged alliances with the National Association for the Advancement of Colored People (NAACP) and the Congress of Industrial Organizations (CIO) to advance civil rights, pushing for anti-lynching laws, abolition of the poll tax (a tool of disenfranchisement in the South during Jim Crow), and fair employment law. Ninety-eight percent of southern whites still supported segregation, and the political door swung wide open again to an acceptance of the Republican party in the South.[78]

---

77. *Tyranny of the Minority* by Steven Levitsky and Daniel Ziblatt; P.95; Crown Publishing, 2023.

78. "Tyranny of the Minority" by Steven Levitsky and Daniel Ziblatt; P.96; Crown Publishing, 2023.

RACIAL CONSERVATISM VERSUS CIVIL RIGHTS

Over the next 30 years, the disparity over social issues grew between the two political parties. In 1948, Harry Truman became the first democratic president to openly embrace civil rights and include a strong civil rights plank in their platform. High-profile racial integration events (1954 *Brown v Board of Education* decision, 1955-56 Montgomery bus boycott, and 1957 deployment of federal troops to integrate Little Rock Central High School) generated widespread southern white resistance. Starting early in the 1960s the Democrats became the party of civil rights attracting many Black voters. Republicans repositioned towards racial conservatism appealing to voters who embraced the status quo of traditional racial hierarchies. Consequently in every presidential election after 1964 the Republicans won the largest share of the white vote.

This strategic decision to move the Republican party in the direction of racial conservatism was based on several facts. Nearly 90 percent of the U.S. population in the 1960s was white. Additionally, public opinion polls showed considerable white anxiety over civil rights both in the South and the North. Most whites in *both* major parties opposed government policies to combat segregation such as busing and affirmative action. 1966 polls showed civil rights as the biggest problem in voters' minds, and 85% of whites surveyed said Blacks were moving "too fast" toward racial equality.[79] The strategy to employ "racial conservatism" was initially effective due to the white backlash to the civil rights movement, but over time that strategy was diminished in its effectiveness.

We are a nation of immigrants and always will be. The difference is initially we were immigrants of the predominately white Anglo-Saxon heritage. Now we are a nation of immigrants from all around the world, and we become darker each year. For example, the last public high school I taught in Accomack County on the Eastern Shore of Virginia was a majority-minority student body with white students comprising only about 30%.

---

79. *Tyranny of the Minority* by Steven Levitsky and Daniel Ziblatt; P.98; Crown Publishing, 2023.

RACIAL CONSERVATISM PLUS FAITH COMMUNITIES

Because of the diminished effectiveness of racial conservatism, the Republican party had to make some adjustments to compensate for the electorate lost to the emerging Democratic Black vote. Consequently, the Republicans adapted their political strategy going forward by incorporating the faith communities in the late 1960s and early 1970s as discussed earlier. This is when the evangelical communities became politically active with the Republican party through organizations like the Moral Majority led by Jerry Falwell, Sr. As mentioned before, I participated in this political action by marching with other members of those faith communities in protests against abortion.

The results of these revised Republican strategies paid electoral dividends. The Republicans won every presidential election between 1968 and 1988 except the 1976 post-Watergate election. In 1994, the Republicans won the House of Representatives for the first time since 1955. By 1995 the Republicans controlled the House, the Senate, and thirty governorships.

This strategy of forming a coalition of white and Christian constituents produced great success through the 1990s for the Republicans. Historians are quick to point out that often what is a political strength turns into a great vulnerability. Such was the case for the Republican party moving into the 21st century. The Republican party found itself captured by a racially conservative base that was shrinking due to the changing demographics of the nation. While Republicans remained overwhelmingly white and Christian into the 21st century, America did not.[80]

THE PARTY OF RACIAL RESENTMENT

Let me pause to underscore the point made above that "the Republican party found itself captured by a racially conservative base."[81] This base

---

80. "Tyranny of the Minority" by Steven Levitsky and Daniel Ziblatt; P.101; Crown Publishing, 2023.

81. Ibid, P.101

turned out to be a growing monster within the party. Surveys taken at the turn of the century indicated that the majority of white Republicans had a high degree of "racial resentment." This resentment was measured by the American National Election Study. Participants in the study were asked to agree or disagree with the following four related statements:

- Blacks should work their way up and overcome prejudice without any special favors like many other minorities.

- Generations of slavery and discrimination make it difficult for Blacks to work their way out of the lower class.

- Blacks have gotten less than they deserve.

- If Blacks would only try harder, they could be as well off as whites.

This study containing these deprecating statements resulted in the high measure of racial resentment that was captured within the Republican party at the turn of the century.[82] That high racial resentment launched the party in a direction that has resulted in some extreme views in the Republican Party today such as inciting an insurrection. Those perspectives have been emboldened gradually over time as the demographics of the nation continue to change in favor of a majority-minority population.

Examples of these demographic trends are as follows. The percentage of non-Hispanic white Americans fell from 88 percent in 1950 to 69 percent in 2000 to 58 percent in 2020. African Americans, Hispanic Americans, and Asian Americans now constituted 40 percent of the country. The percentage of white Americans living in predominately white neighborhoods fell from 78 percent in 1990 to 44 percent in 2020. Intermarriage rates and the percentage of multiracial Americans rose dramatically. America grew markedly less Christian and more religiously diverse. The percentage of Americans identifying as white, and Christian fell from more than 80% in 1976 to 43% in 2016.[83]

---

82. *Tyranny of the Minority* by Steven Levitsky and Daniel Ziblatt; P.100-101; Crown Publishing, 2023.
83. Ibid, P.102

In 2012, for the first time in U.S. History, Black turnout rates exceeded white rates. To adapt to the changing electorate, the leadership of the Republican party tried to steer away from the radicalized path it had embarked on in the late 1960s. The attempt was met with stiff resistance at the grassroots level and was pulling the party in a different direction. The party response in many states was a change to a focus on shrinking the electorate.[84]

In other words, the GOP was facing the dilemma that it was no longer possible to win future elections by winning greater portions of the white, Christian electorate because the demographics were changing too rapidly. Our nation was becoming majority non-white and not Christian. The Republican response was to shrink the overall election pool. In other words, they focused on coming up with some way to eliminate votes either through targeting voters for disqualification or by making it more difficult for selected groups of people to vote. They had a solution; now they were in search of a problem for that solution. The problem was found: voter ID law.[85]

VOTER FRAUD

Lawfare is the use of legal systems and institutions to damage or delegitimize an opponent or to deter an individual's usage of their legal rights. The term may refer to the use of legal systems and principles against an enemy, such as by damaging or delegitimizing them, wasting their time and money.[86] For the purposes of this discussion, lawfare refers to legislation that was created with the intent to combat voter fraud when voter fraud did not exist. In reality, the legislation was designed to dampen turnout among lower-income, minority, and young voters.[87]

---

84. *Tyranny of the Minority* by Steven Levitsky and Daniel Ziblatt; P.108; Crown Publishing, 2023.

85. *Ibid*, P.109

86. Wikipedia; "Lawfare"

87. *Tyranny of the Minority* by Steven Levitsky and Daniel Ziblatt; P.111; Crown Publishing, 2023.

The Justice Department under President George W. Bush launched an unprecedented effort to identify and punish cases of voter fraud between 2002 and 2005. Out of hundreds of millions of votes cast only 35 voters were convicted of fraud. Most of these cases were mistakes or violations that would not have been prevented by a voter ID law. Before 2005, no U.S. state required photo identification to vote. Between 2005 and 2011, only the states of Georgia and Indiana required voter ID. Between 2011 and 2016 13 Republican-led states passed strict photo ID laws combating voter impersonation fraud. Seven of the 11 states with the highest African American turnout in 2008 adopted new voting restrictions after 2010. Nine out of the 12 states with the highest Hispanic population growth between 2000 and 2010 passed restrictive voting laws during the same period. The goal was almost certainly not preventing fraud but aimed at making it harder for Black, Latino, and poorer citizens to vote.[88]

What was an acceptable strategy in the first ten years of the 21st century turned out to be a pivotal Republican strategy in the election of 2020. Claims of voter fraud were being made by President Trump before the election was held. After the election, the campaign for the incumbent President Trump and others filed 62 lawsuits contesting the election process, vote counting, and the vote certification process in nine states and the District of Columbia. All suits were dropped or dismissed due to a lack of evidence and described as frivolous and without merit. In one instance the Trump campaign lost multiple cases in six states on a single day.[89]

When the election results were finalized, President Trump refused to accept them. For the first time in American history, a sitting president refused to accept defeat. Instead, the sitting president waged a 2-month campaign to overturn the election results. In those months the president and his proxies pressured dozens of governors, state election officials, and state legislative leaders to tamper with or undo the results.

---

88. Ibid, P.109-111
89. Wikipedia, "Post election lawsuits related to the 2020 presidential election".

Voter fraud was not responsible for Donald Trump's election, and it was not responsible for the loss of his reelection. But President Trump was about to take this idea of voter fraud to a new level. His actions were to be the impetus that propelled the biggest threat to our democracy to date. Up to that time, claims of voter fraud was a strategy employed by the Republican party to serve as the "shiny object" used to distract from the effort to make voting difficult for Black, Latino, and poorer citizens. In the final analysis, this strategy by the Republican party to suppress the vote was not the fatal threat that almost caused our democracy to fall. The fatal threat was not even President Trump's refusal to accept the election results of 2020. The potentially fatal threat to our democracy was the sanctioning and support of President Trump's efforts by the majority of Republican members of Congress. That enablement by the Republican members of Congress caused President Trump's efforts against our democracy to almost be a fatal blow. January 6, 2021 spouted the perfect political storm.

THE PERFECT POLITICAL STORM

"The Perfect Storm" is a movie released in 2000 based on the 1997 creative non-fiction book of the same name depicting the story of the Andrea Gail, a commercial fishing vessel that was lost at sea with all hands after being caught in the perfect storm of 1991.[90] The actual Perfect Storm that occurred in 1991, also known as The No-Name Storm and the Halloween Gale/Storm, was a nor'easter that absorbed Hurricane Grace and ultimately evolved into a small unnamed hurricane itself late in its life cycle. The 1993 U.S. Coast Guard's investigative report said that *Andrea Gail*, caught in the hurricane, was experiencing 30-foot waves and winds anywhere from 58 to 92 mph around the time of the last communication. The investigative report did, however mention a buoy off the coast of Nova Scotia recording a record wave height of 100.7 feet.[91]

---

90. Wikipedia; "The Perfect Storm" (film)
91. Wikipedia; The Perfect Storm 1991

The political perfect storm that erupted on Jan. 6th was a similar combination of political elements that produced the gale-force political winds over our nation's Capital that almost toppled our democracy. The political elements colliding on the Capitol grounds that day were caused by the influence of a political leader who had sown a spirit of grievance into an attending crowd of citizens, a successful campaign in selling the notion that a fraudulent election had occurred ("the Big Lie"), and a sympathetic political party that enabled a political leader to lead events that fateful day. Let's address each of these political storm elements separately and then discuss the potential implications of their collision to our democracy.

FIRST POLITICAL STORM: A PARTY OF GRIEVANCE

It has been said that Donald Trump did not hijack the Republican Party; he understood it. Trump succeeded in capitalizing on the grievance votes that had been festering in the Republican party since the conclusion of the Civil War when civil rights advocates began to push back against the mistreatment of Black Americans. Trump's unique willingness to say and do things that other Republicans rejected as bigoted, racist, or cruel allowed him to dominate the market for white grievance votes. Trump's campaign signaled to white voters that he intended to maintain the racial hierarchy.[92]

From the founding of America, white Protestants had sat atop a seemingly unmovable racial hierarchy. Positions of power and prestige were occupied, almost without exception, by white protestant men until the 1960s. Every American president, vice president, House Speaker, Senate majority leader, chief justice of the Supreme Court, chairman of the Federal Reserve, and chairman of the Joint Chiefs of Staff was a white man until the late 1980s.

All this changed dramatically in the 21st century. America was no longer overwhelmingly white, and racial hierarchies were weakening.

---

92. *Tyranny of the Minority* by Steven Levitsky and Daniel Ziblatt; P.117; Crown Publishing, 2023.

Challenges to white Americans' long-standing social dominance left many with feelings of alienation, displacement, and deprivation.[93]

I personally believed that electing Barack Obama as our first Black President would bring healing to our country from that "spirit of racism" that has existed in our country since the days of Lincoln. Actually, the exact opposite occurred. That feeling of displacement and deprivation that had been sown in our nation since the turn of the century was targeted by Trump. Trump was able to capitalize on white voter resentment through his rhetoric. Trump had honed his racial rhetoric since initiating his political career with his accusations of President Obama's birth certificate being falsified. Following Obama's eight years of being our first Black President, Trump's grievance message appealed to the racist underbelly of our nation's electorate. That grievance message hit home with many of those who considered themselves aggrieved, four years later when Trump and Pence ran for re-election against the first Black-Asian woman vice presidential candidate. Thus, Trump was the first element of this perfect political storm. He was the perfect candidate for the perfect time.

SECOND POLITICAL STORM: THE BIG LIE

The second storm was the false claim of a fraudulent election. This storm had already existed for many years because the Republican Party had been endorsing the existence of fraudulent elections and the need for strict voter ID laws before Trump. The alleged voter fraud in the 2020 election took on many forms and came to be known as "the Big Lie." As mentioned previously, the courts repeatedly rejected the notion of fraud in the 2020 election.

The Trump presidency left the Republican party deeply immersed in white resentment politics. Replacement theories ran rampant including everything from Jews to Democrats to immigrants used by a cabal of elites who were out to "replace" the white population. By the end of Trump's presidency, fear and resentment had pushed a strikingly large

---

93. Ibid, P.113

number of Republicans toward extremism. "A 2021 survey sponsored by the American Enterprise Institute found that 56% of Republicans agreed with the statement that "the traditional American way of life is disappearing so fast that we may have to use force to save it."[94] The stage was set for an assault on democracy itself.

THIRD POLITICAL STORM: A SYMPATHETIC POLITICAL PARTY

The third component of this perfect storm was a sympathetic political party that enabled Donald Trump. Few principles are more essential to democracy than admitting defeat in a political election. When political parties lose an election, they must be able to recognize their opponent's victory and move on for the sake of our country. That is exactly what Al Gore and the Democratic party did on Nov. 29, 1999, when the vice president conceded to Texas Governor George Bush over the disputed electoral count in Florida. Again, that is what Hillary Clinton and the Democratic party did when conceding to Donald Trump amid high speculation on Russian interference in the results of the 2016 election. It is that cooperative ability of each party that preserves our democracy and its democratic process of elections. If that is lost, our democracy becomes dysfunctional.

It was not simply Trump who refused to accept defeat in the 2020 election. It was the bulk of the Republican party as well. The Republican Accountability Project identified 224 of 261 (86 percent) Republican members of Congress who expressed doubt about the legitimacy of the 2020 election. On January 6, nearly two-thirds of the House Republicans voted against certification of the election results.[95]

Many top Republicans assisted Trump's effort to overturn the election. South Carolina's senator Lindsey Graham, Utah's senator Mike Lee, and Texas's senator Ted Cruz all actively supported Trump's effort

---

94. *Tyranny of the Minority* by Steven Levitsky and Daniel Ziblatt; P.119; Crown Publishing, 2023.

95. *The Republican Accountability Project*. Downloaded from https://accountability.gop.

to overturn the election. Seventeen Republican state attorneys general filed a lawsuit with the Supreme Court seeking to invalidate the results in Georgia, Pennsylvania, Michigan, and Wisconsin. In nine of the most closely fought states, 44% of GOP legislators took steps to "discredit or overturn" the results of the 2020 election. Republican elected officials from both the Federal and State levels overwhelmingly refused to publicly accept the results of the 2020 election.

The second principle of democratic politics is the unambiguous rejection of violence. Trump incited a violent insurrection seeking to block the peaceful transfer of power. He never denounced these actions, only condoned them. Initial Republican leadership criticism from Senator McConnell and House member Kevin McCarthy quickly abated or changed to a tacit approval of Trump. Lynn Cheney was an outspoken critic of Trump and served as Co-chair of the House Impeachment Committee. Consequently, she was ostracized from the Republican party and lost her seat in the House of Representatives. Her loyalty to democracy derailed her political career.

The Republican Accountability Project tried to determine how to characterize the state of the entire Republican party whether it was pro or anti-democratic. The assessors constructed a method to give a "democracy grade" to all members of Congress in 2021 on six criteria based on events that occurred in and around the insurrection on January 6 of that year. The first three questions spoke directly to the principle of accepting the results of the elections. The latter three questions spoke to a willingness to condone extremist violence. More than 60% (161 of 261) of Republican members of Congress adopted undemocratic positions on at least five of the six questions, earning a grade of F. Fifty-four Republicans adopted anti-democratic positions on at least four of the questions. Only 16 Republicans adopted consistently democratic positions and earned an A. By this measure, most Republicans in Congress adopted consistently anti-democratic positions after the 2020 election. Eighty percent adopted mostly anti-democratic positions. Only 6% behaved in a consistently democratic manner, and most retired or lost primaries in 2022.[96]

---

96. *Ibid.*

THE STATE OF OUR DEMOCRACY

A quick review of this chapter will validate the chapter heading. That is, "liberty is under siege" in our nation. Our liberty is under siege because the state of our democracy is fragile. We have not recovered from the assault on our democracy that occurred a few short years ago. The ongoing criminal prosecution of our former president for his involvement in the insurrection in our Capital, and other crimes has only emboldened his attacks on our democracy and resulted in making him the Republican Party nominee for the upcoming presidential election this year. That alone is sufficient to declare a state of emergency for our democracy, but it is not the only reason.

If we were to plot the racial events since the days of Lincoln to the 2021 insurrection and the political responses to them discussed in this chapter in chronological order, we would see an alignment of efforts that have continually undermined our democracy. Since the conclusion of the war that ended slavery in our nation, Americans have purposely targeted Black Americans and other minorities to rob them of their liberties. Those efforts have been directly and indirectly supported by our political system, with parties vying for political dominance. But one party has consistently deferred to a preference for white racism. Following is a graphic portrayal of these highlights in an attempt to clearly show the key aspects of this chapter.

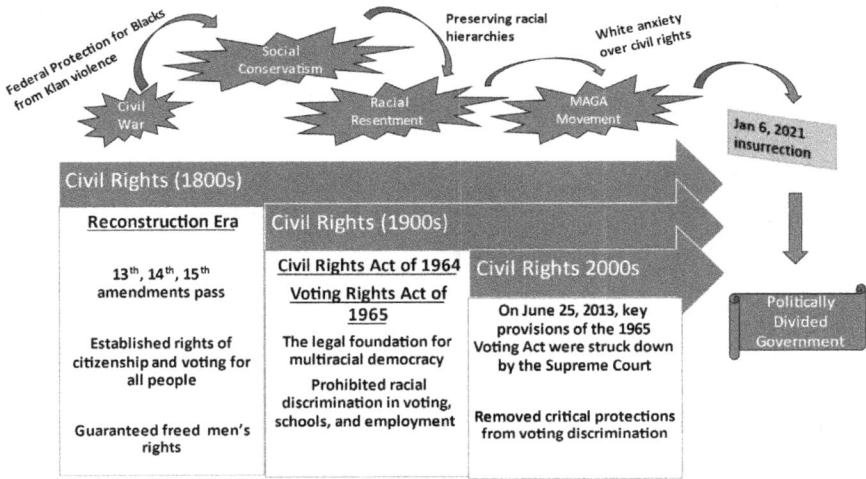

One party has focused on suppressing the liberties of the minority races in our nation. That same party I continued to support through most of my voting years without paying attention to that party's racial priorities. I listened to my faith leaders, not fully understanding their relationship with this party, not realizing I was being manipulated by my faith. I followed my faith, blinded to the moral plight of my fellow Americans of a different race and color. This kind of unquestioning devotion to one party, right or wrong, puts our liberties are under siege and our democracy on unstable ground. This instability in our democracy is not based on any one vote. It is based on the untold number of Americans who are still being manipulated by their faith, their favorite news channel, or their favorite social media.

I offer this analysis in the hope it will sound an alarm to the unaware. It is my attempt to show the direct relationship among all the social-political events that have occurred in our nation since the Civil War and how they all lead like a laser focus to Trump and the events of January 6. There is no coincidence in this alignment. There is a commonality of racism and desire for political control that travels a direct and straight path like an arrow headed for the bull's eye of a target. The arrow is racism in our nation. The target is the dismantling of our democracy.

Our democracy is under siege and will remain so until enough Americans become aware of our dire circumstances. It will require Americans to look a little deeper than the sound bites or visuals offered by social media. Our nation has been captivated by a former game show star who posed as a successful businessman. That same man has now been convicted of fraudulent business practices and is at risk of losing everything. Our nation has been captivated by a politician who promised to make things great again but instead led our nation to the brink of dismantling our democracy. Our nation has been captivated again long enough to entertain the possibility of putting this same man again in charge of the democracy he almost destroyed while promising to dismantle it if he is reelected.

A biblical principle is in play right before our eyes. Paul in his letter to the Galatians offered comfort in perilous times with the words, "Whatever a man sows, that he will also reap." In other words, in the context of our current times, if we re-elect this man to be our leader again, we will get what we deserve. By God's grace, I hope we do not get what we deserve but am resigned to accept it if we do. We have no one to blame but ourselves.

CHAPTER 9

Information Warfare

For several summers while I was still in school, I worked with my father. Born in Brooklyn, New York to a family of Italian immigrants, my dad dropped out of school in the 8th grade to help support his family. It was a time when hard work was more valued than an education, and my father grew up working hard trying to hone different skills. After surviving World War II as an Army medic, he married and settled into his own business of house painting.

Looking back, I cherish those summers now. Not knowing it at the time, those months would turn out to be the most quality hours I would ever spend with my dad. Oddly, one of the clearest memories I have of those days was that my dad always had a cigarette hanging from his lips. He could be 30 feet up in the air on a ladder or walking on a roof, and he would have a stream of smoke trailing behind him. He used to brag that he would smoke a pack of cigarettes a day and had never been sick a day in his life. I remember that to be a generally true statement as he worked six or seven days a week for as long as I can remember. That is until he abruptly died of lung cancer at 54 years old.

Before my father died, a big controversy over the link between smoking and lung cancer was made public. After a long-disputed debate, the cigarette industry was hit with the largest civil fine in US history of $200 billion after which they were allowed to continue sales with new restrictions on advertising.[97]

Regardless of the warnings about cancer, I tried smoking in my early adulthood. I wanted to have that same look as my father as he went about his business, cigarette in his mouth. I identified with that image of a man doing manly things. He seemed to tilt his head and squint his eyes in such a manner that the smoke never impaired his vision. I never mastered the technique but continued to try until my father died. Then, I abruptly quit, never smoking again.

MISINFORMATION VERSUS DISINFORMATION

I continued to smoke cigarettes while there was evidence in the news that it could be hazardous to my health. I believe I continued to smoke, at least in part, because of the *disinformation* that was circulating at the time about the risks.

Merriam-Webster defines disinformation as "false information deliberately and often covertly spread in order to influence public opinion or obscure the truth. Disinformation can also be characterized as targeted manipulation." It is different from *misinformation*. Misinformation is an ordinary misconception.[98] Merriam-Webster defines misinformation as information that is incorrect or misleading. The difference is that misinformation lacks the intention to mislead, whereas disinformation intentionally leads one away from the truth.

For example, when I was a college freshman, I found myself in a state far away from home and knowing very few people. On one occasion, I got the wild idea to embellish my background to a young lady I had just met. To her, I was a surfer from California. That sounded a lot more impressive

---

97. *On Disinformation* by Lee McIntyre; P.10; The MIT Press, 2023.

98. *Ibid.*, P.7.

than being a bad swimmer from New Jersey. That is disinformation. It is the targeted manipulation of false information designed to produce some expected outcome. It also is a very bad way to build a future relationship. When you are an immature adolescent in college like me the damage was limited to my own future relationship with this young lady. But if a corporation or a politician uses disinformation, it can lead to loss of life for many people or a loss of democracy for an entire nation.

STRATEGIC DENIALISM

On December 15, 1953, the heads of the four largest tobacco companies in the United States met with a public relations specialist at the Plaza Hotel in New York City. The purpose of the meeting was to strategize a response to a study about to be made public that drew a link between cigarette smoking and lung cancer. The strategy developed was to fight the science behind the study. The goal was to get the general public to question something that the scientists believed to be true. To accomplish that, the tobacco companies had to hire their own scientists to produce a counter-narrative stressing nothing was yet proven, and the issue was an open scientific debate.[99]

This is the narrative that my father and I chose to believe. I do not remember it being an extended discussion between us or an agonizing decision. It just was part of the common narrative that was in the environment that we chose to accept and believe.

The goal of the tobacco industry's strategy was not to prove that smoking did not cause cancer, it was simply to create enough doubt in the public eye for smokers to continue buying cigarettes. The tobacco companies rode that wave of doubt for 40 years, continuing to profit as the heads of the seven largest tobacco companies testified in a 1994 congressional hearing that nicotine was not addictive. It wasn't until 1998 that they received their record-setting fine after which they were allowed to continue to sell cigarettes with new restrictions on advertising. It

---

99. *On Disinformation* by Lee McIntyre; P.8-9; The MIT Press, 2023.

wasn't until 2004 when a 1969 leaked memo surfaced which proved that industry executives had known all along that their product was deadly. The tobacco companies conducted what is called strategic denialism. [100]

Strategic denialism is a coordinated campaign run by individuals and/or organizations to spread disinformation to large numbers of people with the intent to cause doubt, division, and distrust. Strategic because the information is designed for a targeted audience. The tobacco companies' message was targeted at smokers such as my dad and me. Denialism because the message is crafted to reject any competing narrative to theirs and create an army of deniers. The tobacco industry's strategy was to create enough doubt in the smoker's mind that he would continue to smoke. [101] It certainly worked on me. I remember seeing the surgeon general's warning stamped on the side of the package of cigarettes as I smoked them. The only thing that convinced me and many others to change our views on smoking was watching our loved ones die from lung cancer.

Another example of a recent strategic denial campaign involves the concept of global warming (aka climate change). There have been many works published by journalists and academia demonstrating that the fossil fuel companies' denial of global warming followed the same strategy employed by tobacco companies. Their denialism was a decades-long strategy that included "contrarian" scientific work, Congressional donations, annual conferences hosted by "think tanks" to raise doubt on any scientific consensus, and a public relations program to soften the industry image. It was later revealed through a series of leaked industry memos that the fossil fuel companies had known the truth about global warming as far back as 1977. They continued their denialism over the years while they continued to make a profit.[102]

---

100. *Ibid.*, P.10.

101. *Ibid.*, P.7.

102. *Ibid.*, P.11-12

DISINFORMATION, STRATEGIC DENIAL AND POLITICS

For strategic denialism to be successful, disinformation must be created, amplified, and believed. If the objective of denialism is to continue to make a profit, it is sufficient to simply raise doubt. If the objective of denialism is political, it is not sufficient just to raise doubt, but rather the truth must be replaced with a counter-narrative combined with an environment of distrust.[103]

To create an environment of distrust in political denialism, people must be convinced the opposition is not trustworthy. The strategy must include a narrative that the opposition is deceitful, dishonest, and/or lying. In so doing, it establishes an allegiance to a person, a party, or a cause that is facilitating the denialism. This allegiance is not based on facts; rather, it is based on identity.

Politics thrives on an identity-based allegiance. It divides people according to such allegiances as Republican, Democrat, Independent or something else. Part of our identity becomes our political affiliation. Identity is a powerful force in uniting people. Often, it is more powerful than facts.

Strategic denialism is particularly effective in politics. This is because once an issue is introduced into politics, it is easily exploited by the ill will that exists in partisan politics. For example, if Democrats believe the moon is made out of green cheese, I will probably go along with that belief if I am a Democrat. I may not understand all the reasons behind that claim, but that is acceptable to me because I know Republicans oppose the position.

A common political identity is that Democrats are liberal and Republicans conservative. The truth of that statement depends on the subject. The Democrats are generally more liberal concerning social programs but have demonstrated themselves to be financially conservative relative to fiscal responsibilities like the national debt for the last few

---

103. *Ibid.*, P.22

administrations. This illustrates the point that identity is based more on perceptions than facts.

That is why identity trumps facts (excuse the pun.) It doesn't matter what the facts are, one's identity is established with a particular political party, and that establishes his or her loyalty. It is not necessary to have a good understanding of the facts of an issue. If one side supports a particular issue, the other side is automatically against it.

Many political issues have conducted strategic denial campaigns effectively. Climate change denial became much more effective once it was politicized because it could exploit partisan enmity and not just doubt. The same is true with vaccine denial, election denial, and the entire "Stop the Steal Campaign." When a politician or a political party is successful in getting people to trust information controlled by them and distrust any other information sources as biased or false, they have successfully created a news silo. Information from any other source is fake news, a lie, and biased. Every issue becomes "us against them."[104]

Identity not only trumps facts, but it is even stronger than old friendships, even friendships that formed in the church while serving together for many years. I mentioned previously in this writing spending an afternoon with an old friend whom I had not seen in 15 years. As members of the same church, we had spent much time ministering together. Now we were different people during different political times.

As mentioned before, our visit turned unpleasant when the discussion turned to politics. What was not mentioned was that we could not agree on the facts. He trusted only one news source which identified itself as "fair and balanced." My friend's position was that all other news sources were liberal, biased, and inaccurate. His justification for the claim was that all those liberal news networks said the same thing. The "fair and balanced" source offered a different position. The implication was that those other news sources were conspiring to create a common narrative that had to be false. My friend rationalized that if a news source is unique, it had to be true.

---

104. *Ibid.,* P. 24-25

This is an example of successfully creating a "news silo" to support a denialism campaign. I referred to the scriptural reference for determining the truth as "by the mouth of two or three witnesses" (2 Corinthians 13:1). My friend dismissed it as irrelevant. Political identity is stronger than old relationships. It is even stronger than scriptural references in the minds of those exposed effectively to denialism. It creates an intolerance to opposing views, regardless of the facts.

WE ALL LIE AT TIMES

None of us are without the sin of lying in our lives. For most of us, it is infrequent and without what seems to be for some good cause at the time. For example, when my daughter was very young, she developed a serious case of warts. For no apparent reason, she suddenly broke out with what seemed like dozens of them, varying in size, all over her hands and face. The dermatologist could not explain the cause, but he was certain of the only treatment and that was to freeze them off. It was a relatively painless procedure, but it was terrifying for a 3-year-old to see a cone-shaped object that appeared to be smoking approach her face and hands. It required a concerted effort of a nurse and me to hold this screaming child still enough for the doctor to freeze each wart one at a time. It would require several sessions like this, but the bad news was the doctor could not predict how many sessions it would take to remove all the warts. My little girl was too young to understand why she had to go through this repeated torture, but she was old enough to recognize the neighborhood when we approached the doctor's office for each appointment. Each week, I had to lie to her that we were not going to the doctor. Then, when it was obvious that we were, I had to lie that he wasn't going to do that same procedure. Of course, as soon as she saw that smoking cone in his hand she started screaming "Why, Daddy? Why?" Not sure how many visits it took, but eventually the warts all vanished.

Looking back now, some 40 years later, it seems like I should have been able to come up with a better approach than just lying, but I couldn't think of one then and probably couldn't today in the stress and urgency of the moment. Sometimes, we all just lie because it is convenient and we feel it is necessary for the greater good. However, that is not what this chapter is about. This is about deliberate lying for the explicit benefit of a few, regardless of the cost.

That is why I characterize denialism as an insidious evil. It is insidious because it does its harm slowly and largely unnoticed on the surface of everyday life. Evil because it does unrepairable harm to an untold number of lives. I believe my father was shocked when he was diagnosed with lung cancer and had just a few weeks to live. He told no one—just went about his business trying to put his affairs in order the best he could in silence. He believed the disinformation just as I had. The only difference was that his death revealed the truth to me.

Likewise, this insidious evil of denialism has currently infected our nation. Because it is insidious, it continues to work slowly, slightly below the surface of our society, generally unnoticed by the masses. It is evil because we have yet to experience the full extent of its harm and to determine the fullness of its outcome. Let me explain.

DENIALISM AN INSIDIOUS EVIL

"Stop the Steal" is an active strategic denialism campaign. Even though the election that was the subject of the steal occurred more than three years ago, the campaign remains as relevant today and to the future of our democracy as ever.

To the casual observer, the call to stop the certification of the 2020 election on January 6, 2021, was unsuccessful. The courts confirmed and Congress certified the election. The rioters were unsuccessful in their attempts to confront Nancy Pelosi or Mike Pence. There was no coup. Joe Biden was duly sworn in as the current President of the United States.

However, as a strategic denialism campaign, "Stop the Steal" still is very effective. "Sixty-six percent of Republican voters still think the 2020 election was stolen and that Trump is the rightful president. A stunning

147 Republican members of Congress still refuse to publicly acknowledge that Joe Biden is the legitimately elected president of the United States."[105]

The biggest threat from "Stop the Steal" is the realization that the campaign was not merely an attempt to overturn the last election but also an effort to affect all future elections, by undermining voters' confidence in future presidential elections. If voter confidence can be undermined to the extent that voters believe a fair election does not exist, then voters will believe that not only the next election but any that follows can be stolen. If so, the bedrock of our democracy has been made unstable. There is a crack in the foundation of our democracy that, if it structurally fails, will eliminate any guarantee for a safe and secure process to determine who will lead our nation. That leaves the door wide open for an autocratic leader to step in and dismantle our democracy. As the current presidential election is in full swing, the Republican candidate for president continues to spew election lies continuously. His message of retribution, punitive justice, and destruction of the radicals that oppose him continues to be embraced by approximately half of the electoral base.

This type of strategizing goes beyond politics. It is morally reprehensible. Associated actions arise from actual or imputed bad character. That is Merriam-Webster's definition of evil. That is why I characterize this denialism as an insidious evil. Left unchecked, the dismantling of our democracy could occur during our generation, right before our eyes.

INFORMATION WARFARE: A WAR OF WORDS

We are living through a time when a battle of words is being waged. We have opposing forces launching narratives that in some cases are untethered to reality. It is a war that is no longer just information but also includes the common mistakes of misinformation intermingled with the assaults of disinformation. Added to the battle is the world of political spin that eliminates normal reasoning from the discussion. A case in

---

105. *Ibid.*, P. 27-28

point is a recent judicial ruling being appealed to the Supreme Court of the State of Colorado.

Donald Trump's attorneys argued an appeal against the recent court decision that found Trump guilty of leading an insurrection on January 6, 2021. The argument made was that the 14th Amendment of the Constitution doesn't disqualify him from running for reelection because Section 3 of the amendment disqualifies insurrectionists who have "previously taken an oath …. to "support" the Constitution. The argument in his appeal is that he is eligible for the presidency again in 2024 because he swore to "preserve, protect, and defend" the Constitution, not to "support" it.

Of course, the words "preserve, protect, and defend" have a different meaning than the word "support." They reflect a higher degree of protection and personal involvement than the word "support." I "support" my favorite sports team. I will fight with every bit of my ability to "preserve, protect, and defend" my wife and family. That wholehearted pledge to "preserve, protect, and defend" includes an implicit guarantee to "support" as well. To imply anything different is just silly. What is more, it is common sense that when the founding fathers carefully chose those words "preserve, protect, and defend" it would be naturally assumed it meant to "support" as well.

Yet, these are the arguments that are being made before a federal court with the intent to dismiss the charges of a former president for leading an insurrection against the United States. The heart of the argument challenges the literal wording of the Fourteenth Amendment, Section Three, of our United States Constitution while ignoring the obvious intent of the founding fathers. The intent was to permanently disbar anyone from the office of the presidency who failed in his or her protection of the Constitution. No matter what words one uses to describe Mr. Trump's actions on that day he did not honor that solemn obligation.

The Supreme Court decided to rule in Mr. Trump's favor based on their interpretation of the Constitution and the rights of a State, in this case Colorado. The Supreme Court decided the State did not have the authority to determine if a candidate was qualified to run for the presidency. While the argument made by Trump's attorneys did not directly affect the ruling, it can be surmised that it created enough uncertainty in the court's deliberations that the justices searched for a way to reject the state's position. This amounts to a very successful war on words.

However, this war of words has long been a part of our history and the 14th Amendment starting with its inception. Although slavery had been eliminated by the Civil War most Southerners firmly held the belief that Black people were meant to be subjugated to the demands of Whites. It was also firmly believed at that time that insurrection posed a viable threat to the survival of the United States as a Republic. Concerning this continued threat of subjugation to Blacks and the possibility of insurrection, Frederick Douglas fought back the way he knew best with words. He was quoted as having no illusions about the persistence of the "malignant Spirit" of the "traitors" that would be passed "from sire to son" and "it will not die out in age." This was the context in which the 14th Amendment was created. The amendment was to protect Black people from the return to subjugation and to protect the nation against insurrection.[106]

Douglas' words were as true then as they are today. Words fostering a spirit of insurrection and subjugation of a people still exist in our nation today at its highest levels of authority. That point gets to the heart of the war on words we find ongoing in our nation. I refer to it as "information warfare." It is a battle of words, but it is a spiritual war whose object is to reach the hearts and minds of the people of our nation.

We as a people are generally uninformed and unaware of the details of our nation. A poll conducted by Pew Research from September 25th to October 1st of this year revealed that 32% of Americans between the ages 18 to 29 regularly get their news from TikTok. It also determined that in 2023 approximately 14% of U.S. adults get their news from TikTok compared to 3% in 2020. This by no means is an extensive analysis but

---

106. "U.S. courts are afraid of the radical 14th Amendment" by Sherrilyn Ifill; *The Washington Post*; Sunday, November 26, 2023; P.21.

it does indicate that if these trends are close to being accurate for the general population it means we are vastly ill-equipped to deal with this information warfare in which we find ourselves in our nation today.

CHAPTER 10

In God We
No Longer Trust

On July 30, 1956, President Dwight D. Eisenhower signed into law the declaration, "In God We Trust," to be the nation's official motto. This law also mandated that the phrase be printed on all American paper currency. Two years earlier, President Eisenhower reflected his feelings concerning inserting the phrase "under God" into the pledge of allegiance in a speech given on Flag Day in 1954. He stated, "In this way, we are affirming the transcendence of religious faith in America's heritage and future; in this way, we shall constantly strengthen those spiritual weapons which forever will be our country's most powerful resource in peace and war."[107]

These words by President Eisenhower reflect the precise reason freedom of religion is such an important component and guarantee of our constitution. Faith, which is the product of our religion, allows us to experience the intersection of the supernatural (God) with the natural (us). We are able to experience the empowerment of daily living through

---

107. www.history.com/this-day-in-history/president-eisenhower-signs-in-god-we-trust-into-law

the lens of faith for clarity of purpose and the courage to pursue the greater good for one another and our nation.

I was four years old when President Eisenhower made that Flag Day speech, much too young to understand any concept of what he was talking about. However, if I had heard the President of the United States approximately a quarter century later describing the spiritual weapons of our faith as our country's most powerful resource in peace and war, I would have shouted a loud "Amen!" That is what Baptist Evangelical Christians did at that time to affirm our agreement with a public statement made by a preacher or a noted speaker like the president. Also, at that time I was familiar with the expression "In God We Trust" because it was on our currency for as long as I could remember. During that same season of my life, we were taught to believe that motto on our currency and engraved on the buildings in Washington, D.C. were evidence that our founding fathers intended our country to be a Christian nation. That was my experience in the evangelical Christian church in the 1980s; however, I later learned that many of those efforts were done with political motives in mind.

Currently, there is a movement in our nation that holds the same beliefs that I experienced in those early evangelical days. Many years ago, those beliefs were not identified as a movement. They were simply stated by Evangelical Christian church leaders as the intended design of our nation by our founding fathers and somehow, we had gone adrift from those original intentions. The message at that time was communicated with an attitude of despair over the spiritual direction of our country. Those same sentiments are being expressed today by certain political leaders. The current Speaker of the House of Representatives recently wrote the following. "Our culture has fallen so far since the founding of our country, and it's just getting worse. I fear America may be beyond redemption."[108]

---

108. "Speaker Mike Johnson frets high schoolers increasingly identify as LGBTQ in friendly email: 'We have much to repent for'"; by Bryan Metzger; *Insider.com*; Dec.5, 2023.

SEPARATION OF CHURCH AND STATE

Almost half of a century has passed since my early Baptist days, and the newly elected speaker of the House of Representatives is reported to have strong ties to Christian nationalism. Christian nationalism is a movement that believes the U.S. is a solely Christian nation and its laws and government should be focused on religion's values.[109] Wikipedia defines Christian nationalism as type of religious nationalism affiliated with Christianity that primarily focuses on the internal politics of society. It has a focus on legislation, both civil and criminal law, which reflects proponents' views of Christianity and the role of religion in political and social life.

Since those early days of my faith experience, I have learned the meaning of the term *separation of church and state*. It is a term commonly used when referring to the First Amendment of our Constitution that reads in part as follows: "Congress shall make no law respecting an establishment of religion or prohibiting the free exercise thereof; ...." Our founding fathers wrote this amendment based on their experiences with a state-sponsored church. Their vision for our nation was to not have that same experience.

The term *separation of church and state* was derived from another term coined by Thomas Jefferson: *wall of separation between church and state*. It is a concept for defining political distance in the relationship between religious organizations and the state. The term also refers to the creation of a secular state and to disestablishing a formal relationship between the church and the state. The concept was promoted by famous philosophers like John Locke during the Age of Enlightenment in Europe in the 17th and 18th centuries.[110]

How the Christian nationalism movement has reached such high levels of influence today is an extended discussion beyond the scope of this book. This infusion of influences, including Christian nationalism,

---

109. "Mike Johnson's Ties to Christian Nationalism Revealed"; *Newsweek Daily Bulletin*; Oct.26, 2023.

110. Wikipedia, "Separation of church and state."

was briefly introduced in Chapter 6 with my references to the writing of Russell Moore's *Losing Our Religion*. Moore writes extensively about the effect these influences have had on the collective faith of our nation and concludes:

> The very *populist* and entrepreneurial energies that led American evangelical Christianity to grow into a world-influencing movement and into a powerful political influence bloc seemed to be what was *now undoing us, right down to friendships of decades.*[111]

I know this experience to be true. That is, I have also experienced an *"undoing"* of previously known friendships and relationships that were at one time based on a commonality of faith. Now that common denominator of faith has been strained and twisted to contort to different *populist* politics and has strained those relationships once held dear. This experience has been repeated several times in recent years resulting in less personal contact, and more distance in those relationships. This has occurred with members of my family, a family both by birth and by faith. In that experience, it feels like we are becoming more isolated and divided with each passing day. Suddenly we begin to understand how a nation can become so isolated and divided that people are willing to take up arms against one another. American against American, friend against friend, family member against family member.

AN OLD STRATEGY FOR A NEW GENERATION

Moore's writing alludes to the not-so-subtle shift in the methodology of the evangelical faith communities in our nation. What was by taught Christian leaders years ago as an intent of our founding fathers to make us a Christian nation is now employed as Christian nationalism being infused at our highest levels of government. This shift to being a powerful political presence started years ago with evangelical leaders

---

111. *Losing Our Religion* by Russell Moore; P. 12; Penguin Random House, 2023.

influencing the faith community to move support away from an evangelical who occupied the White House (Carter) and to an actor-turned-politician (Reagan) over issues like prayer in schools. Then the current administration was perceived as abandoning critical issues such as banning abortion, defending school prayer, and opposing gay rights. That same effort has grown in its sophistication by pivoting to popular issues like anti-immigration and anti-critical race theory while still supporting anti-abortion and anti-gay rights efforts. The strategy is a dated one, going back to before the Civil War, where the confluence of faith and politics dominated society.

To reach the extremes of where we are today, Moore questions the fundamental methods employed over the years and suggests they may have allowed our faith communities to be easily influenced—an influence that suggests less trust in God and more in the current methods of "doing church."

A MARKET-DRIVEN APPROACH

Moore talks about today's market-driven approach to ministry. There is a tendency for pastors to avoid controversial subjects. Positions that may impact attendance or financial support. To do that there is a tendency to define those sins most hated by God as those that least tempt the members. This market-driven approach to ministry will lead to the same approach to the truth[112].

For example, I was part of a denomination that encouraged no alcohol consumption. One Sunday we were visited by a pastor who mentioned the hypocrisy of embracing that position while ignoring the habit of many who overeat at food bars. He was not invited back to our church.

Moore is comparing the process in which evangelical churches grow into a business that adjusts its strategies according to what the consuming market will bear. In other words, give customers what they want so they

---

112. *"Losing Our Religion"* by Russell Moore; P. 12; Penguin Random House, 2023.

keep coming back. While it is good for business, Moore points out that strategy allows what he calls "hypocrites and hucksters" to enter and control the outcome of a faith community.

The market is extremely competitive in the evangelical communities of faith today. The sheer number of churches and varieties of denominations allow people of faith to pick and choose the church of their choice based on the services provided. Churches do many good things, providing community while nurturing the spirit and soul of each person. But Moore's point is that each church must strive to keep its share of the market or else it will have to close its doors. Many churches turn to daycare and/or Christian education to help a church's financial viability. These are good valuable services to a faith community.

The point that Moore is making, however, is that the cost of doing church with a "market-driven" approach is the compromising of the message that is required. This is what Moore means when he asserts that sins become reprioritized by those that least tempt a church's members considered most hateful to God and popular sins are redefined and even sanctified. In other words, churches generally do not focus on those issues that make the majority uncomfortable. The general rule is not to be controversial but to stick to emphasizing the sins that are easily accepted by the church. Moore states that churches generally don't talk about the issues that are higher on God's list of concerns for people of faith. So, what are those things?

It might be difficult to discern which sins are worse than others except for the existence of specific scriptural references listing what "God hates" and calls "abominations." Such a list is found in Proverbs 6:16-19. This list of seven things includes "the shedding of innocent blood", "devising wickedness", and "being attracted to evil." These things seem like they should top any list of heavenly violations, but they do not. The top two listed are "a proud look" and "a lying tongue." Occupying seventh place on the list is "one who sows discord among the brethren."

Over the 30 years of my ministry experience in evangelical communities of faith, including seven years of pastoring my church, I never heard a sermon preached on sins number one, two, or seven. That includes my preaching as well. Why is that? Because it has been my experience that the average church is filled with all three of these issues. All pastors know if they were to address these issues attendance would radically drop. Consequently, no one addresses those sins because that is the last thing any pastor using a market-driven approach wants to happen.

We talk about the shedding of innocent blood all the time in the context of abortion. We will even organize protest rallies in the name of God against abortion. But I have never heard or spoken about the endless slaughter of children in our nation by automatic weapons. Why is that? It is because abortion has been politicized by the evangelical communities of faith and automatic weapons have not. This is what Moore is talking about when he states, sins that are the most popular become redefined and even sanctified. This is a market-driven church philosophy. The consequence is the church being filled with "hypocrites and hucksters."

THE "HYPOCRITES" AMONG US

I have been a hypocrite for most of my years while faithfully ministering in several evangelical churches including while pastoring my church. Of course, not intentionally. I can honestly say I served my faith communities and lived my life of faith as openly and honestly as I knew how with complete transparency—until God opened my eyes to reveal to me the things I had hidden in the recesses of my heart.

I am personally against abortion and have participated in many marches against it, but God softened my heart and my attitude toward it, as shared earlier in this book, first by hearing the pain of others who have gone through it while I was a pastor and second by gently reminding me that I once was implicated in an abortion as a young man. It was only by God's grace that the woman turned out not to be pregnant.

I had been involved in marriage counseling ministries for many years before pastoring for seven years. During all that time I was sympathetic to all those who asked for counsel, but I did so with an attitude in my heart that I was somehow above that kind of behavior. God knew I was not. Years after I was done pastoring, God reminded me how I was prepared to pay for an abortion until it was revealed it was a false alarm. God chose to remind me of my hypocrisy years after my marching and public protesting against abortion. Long after the names of those counseled were forgotten. Now I am geographically relocated and find it impossible to retrace my steps, track down, and make amends in some fashion to those to whom I ministered over the years on this subject. Perhaps the memory was just stuffed away in the recesses of my heart buried under all the holy pride I could muster until I could no longer. I finally felt like the hypocrite that I was and am today unable to confess my sin to those I offended with my pride.

There are things in all our lives that are hidden in the dark areas of our souls, and they elude the light of God. By that I mean over time we tend to compartmentalize events of our lives. We bury the unpleasant experiences in our hearts and consciously try to move on from the pain. Over time, the event is forgotten buried under a ton of new life experiences until the light of God reveals them again hidden away in the dark recesses of our souls. It is not a pleasant experience to see the ugliness within us, but it is healing and liberating when these things are finally exposed and "seen" under God's healing light. My issue is not with the church hypocrites, for we are many. That is an issue that must be reconciled personally by each individual with his or her faith and the God of his or her understanding. My issue is with the "hucksters" in the church. And many surround us.

"HUCKSTERS" ALL AROUND US

Merriam-Webster defines a "huckster" as a "hawker" or "peddler" or one who sells or advertises something in an aggressive, dishonest, or annoying way. A "huckster" can also be defined as one who produces promotional material for commercial clients, especially for radio or television. We have the influences of both types of "hucksters" in our churches today because of the many advanced social platforms and the confluence of faith and politics.

Pastor Moore was a Southern Baptist denominational leader. He describes when his leadership perspective began to change.

> I found myself sitting, sometimes for eight hours at a time, with Southern Baptists like me in heresy trials at which I was not the inquisitor I had been trained to be but the defendant. I hadn't changed my theology, or my behavior, at all. What I had done, as the president of my denomination's public policy agency, was refused to endorse Donald Trump.[113]

Moore goes on to describe the continued chastisement from other leaders of the denomination, trying to bring him back into the fold. One leader told him "We can't get rid of you. All our wives and kids are with you, but we can do psychological warfare until you think twice before you open your mouth." Another friend and respected Baptist leader called to tell him the following. "This is not how you play the game. You give them 90 percent of the red meat they expect, then you can do the 10 percent of side stuff that you want to do, on immigrants or whatever."[114]

As a member of a faith community, we look to our leaders to guide the development and care of our faith. They help us understand and apply scriptural principles to our lives based on their qualifications, their skills, and usually their years of experience. It is unconscionable to think our respected leaders are intentionally misguiding us, but some do. Some are "hucksters." (The church is also influenced by the "hucksters" outside the church.)

The influence of "hucksters" is pervasive in the evangelical church. The receipt of disinformation through our preferred news silos empowers "hucksters" in the pulpits to aggressively promulgate the latest threat to our faith. The temptation to utilize social media to launch a church into the national news brings out the "huckster" in many pastors. A writing by Tim Alberta investigated this phenomenon of the "huckster" in the local evangelical church throughout our nation but he described it by a different name.

113. *Losing Our Religion* by Russell Moore; P. 6; Penguin Random House, 2023.
114. *Ibid*, P.6-7

"HUCKSTERS" AND A CRAVEN RELIGION

"The Kingdom, the Power, and the Glory" describes the results of dozens of interviews by Alberta conducted over four years, investigating what he refers to as "the craven religion" that seems to be consuming evangelical churches throughout our nation.[115] In scores of towns across the country, Alberta encountered evangelicals who believed their religion is under siege. For example, he was told by one church member that he believed there's evidence that the Biden administration has weaponized the Internal Revenue Service to come after churches although no evidence was presented. Alberta concludes that many pastors embrace far-right militarism because their congregants demand it or reward it. Robert Jeffress, pastor of the prominent First Baptist Church of Dallas, initially catapulted to celebrity when he made a ruckus about children's books depicting gay couples in 1998. Bill Bolin, a pastor in Michigan, vaulted to national prominence when he refused to shutter services during the pandemic. Greg Locke, a Tennessee preacher, went viral with a selfie video outside his local Target, skewering the company's policies regarding bathrooms and gender identities. These are only a few anecdotal examples of Alberta's investigation. He concludes that American evangelicalism is in crisis. Instead of fixing on the unseen, there is an obsession with a worldly identity. [116]

EVANGELICALS OF TODAY

In Moore's statement concerning the "market-driven" approach of the evangelical church, he concluded that this type of approach "gives rise to a market-driven approach to truth." This is a fair assessment of the Evangelical church today. What is the standard of truth employed in this community of faith is based on what the market will stand to hear. Any departure from a particular faith community's subset of beliefs is not

---

115. *The Kingdom, The Power, and The Glory* by Tim Alberta; P.13; *Harper Collins; 2023.*
116. *Ibid.*

acceptable as truth. Any information provided outside the selected news silo is fake and not acceptable as truth.

Moore states, "*Evangelical* is just a word we impose artificially to describe a particular type of Christian. No one signs up at a central office to be an "evangelical." And most evangelicals don't identify as evangelicals. They might use words like *saved* or *born again* or *Bible-believing Christian*. This fuzzy term is an attempt to categorize a chaotic and contradictory cast of characters, who often have little in common except for a few emphases and aspirations."[117]

King David the psalmist writes "Some trust in chariots, and some in horses; But we will remember the name of the Lord our God." (Psalm 20:7) King David, the Commander of armies, would know about the limitations of trusting in chariots and horses. He elected to put his trust in God. So that is the question that each evangelical must answer for himself or herself. Do we trust in the news we hear, the political leader we follow, the pastor we listen to, the person next to us in the pew, or do we trust in God? More often than not, one will hear conflicting things from each of these sources. My observation would be that today we very seldom trust in God. Quite often God is the last source we check, if at all. In that case, we can say "In God we no longer trust," no matter what it says on our currency or our official national motto.

---

117. *Losing Our Religion* by Russell Moore; P. 14; Penguin Random House, 2023.

PART 3

WHEN LIBERTY
ENSLAVES:
LET FREEDOM RING

CHAPTER 11

Evangelicals—
Who Are They?

I lost my aunt during the early stages of the recent COVID pandemic. After many years of separation, we had reconciled only a few years before her death. The last time I remember seeing my aunt before our reconnection was at my father's funeral in September 1975. It was as if a lifetime had passed, a period of almost a half-century between my dad's death and seeing my Aunt Sissy again. One of the serendipities in our reconnection was a trove of photos from my childhood which I now cherish dearly.

These photos are of many events in the lives of my family members. Included are several taken the day I made my first communion in the Catholic church. Seeing these pictures, I recalled all the pomp and circumstance through the eyes of a young Catholic child involved in what was a special day. I was appropriately dressed for the ceremony in my all-white suit, white silk bow tie with matching armband, and white shoes. We had rehearsed for weeks every last detail of the day. Despite all the rehearsals, I remember being filled with anxiety during the ceremony.

As we were waiting to enter the school chapel, I noticed the other boys had a small pin on their lapels. I remember being worried that my first communion may not be official if I did not have my pin on my lapel. After the ceremony, I quietly told my mother my deep concern over my missing pin and the legitimacy of my first communion which had just been completed. My mom just smiled, pulled out my pin that had been tucked away in the little prayer missal I was carrying, and pinned it on my lapel. She said now I was just like all the others, and everything was ok. I was very relieved. My mom's validation was enough to satisfy me and my faith at the time.

OUR FOUNDATIONS OF FAITH

The foundations of our faith are formed during the early stages of our lives. My early life experience happened to be immersed in the Catholic Church. Naturally, the initial construct of my faith centered around Catholicism which held until my early adult years. This is a common experience regardless of the type of church or faith. It also applies if one has no exposure to any church or faith. We all form our basic view of God and form a relationship with God based on that initial understanding. That experience will define our view of life and our faith going forward. Even in the cases where there is little exposure to church or faith, we all have an innate sense that God exists, and we adapt our faith accordingly. Atheists and agnostics are simply exercising their faith that God does not exist or their lack of knowledge of God's existence. Some would say that takes more faith than admitting God exists.

BUILDING ON OUR FOUNDATIONS OF FAITH

I was raised in an Italian Catholic family which included my extended family being mostly Catholic as well. Consequently, most of my 12 cousins and their families are practicing Catholics today, some more active in their faith than others. A few of us have ventured into Protestantism.

This is the natural course of faith as taught by Jesus in His parables of the Sower recorded in the gospels of Mathew 13, Mark 4, and Luke 8.

That is to say that the faith experience is different in each person. The above-referenced parable refers to how some seeds grow and flourish, others are constrained for environmental reasons, and some produce nothing. That is true to each one's faith experience: some flourish, some are constrained because of various reasons, and some are rendered idle over time. All experiences of faith are valid.

Often our faith foundations constrain our acceptance of other views of faith and limit the experiential growth of our faith. For example, as a young Catholic boy I was taught the one true Church was the Catholic church. When I converted to Protestantism as a Baptist, I was taught Catholics were not "saved" and Pentecostals were "deceived." As a Pentecostal, I learned there were both Pentecostal Catholics and Pentecostal Baptists. As I added a new construct to my Catholic foundation of faith, I accepted other views of faith and new faith experiences. It required a breaking of former constructs of faith.

DEFINING EVANGELICALS IN THE PAST

I do not remember exactly when I first heard the term "evangelical" Christian, but I do remember I was pastoring at the time. I presumed the term related to Jesus' command to His disciples (Mathew 28:19,20) to "make disciples of all nations, baptizing them" and "teach them to observe all things that I have commanded you." These verses are often referred to as the Great Commission to go out and "evangelize" the world. For the most part, this served as my definition of an "evangelical."

When I pastored, I was a licensed and ordained minister in the International Pentecostal Holiness Church (IPHC) and agreed to follow those commands of Christ as key tenets of our denomination. We considered ourselves to be an "evangelical" denomination. All the protestant denominations that I belonged to during my 30 years of ministry also agreed to those commands of Christ as key tenets of our various denominations. Those various denominations were all considered to be "evangelical" denominations. It was not until recently, many years after pastoring, that I read the definition of an "evangelical" as follows:

> In 1989, a British scholar named David Bebbington posited that evangelicals were distinct because of four principal characteristics: Biblicism (treating scripture as the essential word of God); Crucicentrism (stressing that Jesus's death makes atonement for mankind possible); Conversionism (believing that sinners must be born again and continually transformed into Christlikeness); and Activism (sharing the gospel as an outward sign of that inward transformation). This framework—now commonly called the "Bebbington quadrilateral"—was widely embraced, including by the National Association of Evangelicals. But it also drew its share of criticisms. Efforts to formulate a more effective definition have failed time and again. To the present day, there remains no real consensus around what it means to be an evangelical.[118]

The described "Bebbington quadrilateral" was adhered to by every protestant denominational church that I have been affiliated with over the life of my ministry experience. Treating the Bible as literally "the word of God" (Biblicism), Christ's death on the cross as the blood atonement for our sin (Crucicentrism), the "born again" experience (Conversionism), and sharing the gospel with others (Activism) have been critical components of the life flow of every church to which I have belonged (including the church I pastored) since I left the Catholic church. Consequently, the earlier quoted statement "To the present day, there remains no real consensus around what it means to be an evangelical" gave me great concern. I came to realize that my experience as an "evangelical" is quite different from the experience of an "evangelical" of others, especially compared to those of today.

---

118. *The Kingdom, The Power, and The Glory* by Tim Alberta; P. 10-11; Harper Collins Publishers, 2023.

The Book of Proverbs has proven to me to be a time-tested source of comfort and direction throughout my faith journey. In this case, one of my favorite proverbs helps me with the current debate defining an "evangelical" today. Proverbs 4:7 states "Wisdom is the principal thing; Therefore, get wisdom. And in all your getting, get understanding."

Wisdom is the ability to have insight, good sense, and/or good judgment. Understanding is the ability to comprehend the general relationships of an issue. In other words, this ancient proverb is saying to make good judgments, one must be aware of the context or the environment surrounding the issue to be judged. The classic biblical illustration of this principle is that of King Solomon ordering a baby to be split in half to settle the argument between two women, each claiming to be the mother of the child. Of course, King Solomon was able to identify the true mother by her willingness to give the child away to spare the life of her baby. (1 Kings 3:24-26) That is wisdom with understanding.

This is a critical point when it comes to understanding the definition of "evangelicals" today. We must understand the context or the environment of today to make an accurate judgment about those Christians to whom we assign the label of "evangelical." The context and the environment of today are much different from that when I ministered. That is why I must turn to others familiar with the current "evangelical" environment to explain "who these people are."

DEFINING EVANGELICALS TODAY

Tim Alberta is a staff writer for *The Atlantic* and the former chief political correspondent for *Politico*. The son of an evangelical pastor, Alberta was raised in the church and has spent four years embedded inside the modern evangelical movement trying to answer the question "Who are these people?" He states,

> I toured half-empty sanctuaries and standing-room-only auditoriums; I shadowed big-city televangelists and small-town preachers and everyday congregants. I reported from inside hundreds of churches, Christian colleges,

religious advocacy organizations, denominational nonprofits, and assorted independent ministries. Each of these experiences offered a unique insight into the deterioration of American Christianity.[119]

Alberta announces the conclusion of his extensive effort with that opening proclamation. In his introductory remarks of this impassioned investigation of the only faith he has ever known, he concludes that American Christianity is in "deterioration." The "deterioration" referred to is the radical change he observed in the "evangelical" church from the one he knew in the past. He traces the change beginning to a time before my immersion into the evangelical church:

> By the 1980s, with the rise of the Moral Majority, a religious marker was transforming into a partisan movement. "Evangelical" soon became synonymous with "conservative Christian" and eventually with "white conservative Republican."[120] He then proceeds to illustrate that point with several hundred pages of anecdotal evidence.

It would be folly for me to try and cover all the details of Alberta's exhaustive research in this writing. I do recommend his work, *The Kingdom, the Power, and the Glory: American Evangelicals in an Age of Extremism*," as a thorough analysis to be considered. However, I will mainly focus on those portions of his research that are salient to my personal experiences, with one exception of note that serves to answer the question of this chapter "Who are the evangelicals of today?"

BLENDING FAITH AND POLITICS

As mentioned before, my affiliation with various "evangelical" communities of faith spanned approximately 30 adult years. That period

---

119. *Ibid.,* P. 13.
120. *Ibid,* P.11

includes the time when I was an active member learning, serving, and financially supporting a local church and its associated denomination. It should be noted that the rise of the evangelical community as a political force started long before my immersion into that community and has continued to the current day,10+ years after my departure. Alberta's work has helped me fill in my informational gaps to better understand the circumstances in our nation today.

My involvement in the ministry of Jerry Falwell, Sr. began in 1982. The story of the founding of Thomas Road Baptist Church and Lynchburg Baptist College (later to be renamed Liberty University), both in Lynchburg, Virginia, was part of my local church folklore in Alexandria, Virginia, a 3½ car ride north of Lynchburg. By the time I was involved, Liberty University was a fully accredited university, where I later attained a Master of Arts in Religion with a minor in counseling.

In the summer of 1976, Lynchburg Baptist College was being renamed Liberty Baptist College and a blockbuster event was held on July Fourth to commemorate the nation's bicentennial. More than 25,000 people swarmed the open pastureland. The famed fundamentalist preacher and mentor to Falwell, B.R. Lakin declared to the crowd that another Great Awakening could be at hand. Falwell, on the other hand, warned the crowds America was under assault from secular liberal elites and godless government bureaucrats. Thus, nothing was a given; nothing was promised, and so Christians needed to start fighting back. "The nation was intended to be a Christian nation by our founding fathers," Falwell thundered. "This idea of religion and politics don't mix was invented by the devil to keep Christians from running their own country!"[121]

It is very disheartening to me to read that the roots of today's Christian Nationalism movement started in the confines of my earliest experiences in the evangelical community of faith. These Falwell proclamations of many years ago have taken root and are currently supported by some of the highest-positioned members of our elected government. Speaker of the House of Representatives, Mike Johnson, is an adjunct professor with

121. *Ibid.*, P. 53, 57.

the Helms School of Government at Liberty University. As the speaker, Mr. Johnson is third in line to assume the presidency in the event of a national emergency after the vice president. Johnson is an evangelical conservative who had forged close ties with Christian nationalists such as David Barton, whose writings claiming the country's founders intended to create a Christian nation have been widely debunked by religious scholars.[122]

Mike Johnson, presiding as Speaker of the House, illustrates the political evolution "evangelicals" have experienced over the last several decades as described by Alberta. That is, what started as "evangelicals" being known as "conservative Christians" have moved on to be known as "white conservative Republicans." This evolution is the fruit of mixing politics with faith, which was Falwell's intent from his early days of pastoring.

Falwell was an apolitical pastor in the beginning. In 1958, for example, he took issue with the *Brown v. Board of Education* Supreme Court decision of 1954. He claimed that "the devil himself" was pushing integration and that "the true Negro" did not want it. 'What will the integration of the races do to us?' Falwell asked his all-white congregation. 'It will destroy our race eventually.'"[123]

Over time, Falwell tempered his message and selectively chose his issues. He aligned himself with Senator Joe McCarthy, alerting his church to the risks of communist infiltration. He chastised Martin Luther King for having "left-wing associates." He later retracted his comments about segregation and race, referring to it as a "false prophecy" and welcomed Black families into his church. By the mid-1970s, there was no use in trying to separate politics and theology. In fact, Falwell realized, that combining the two might be the way to save both the country and his upstart college.[124]

---

122. "House speaker's Christian nationalist ties spark first amendment fears"; by Peter Stone; *The Guardian*; December 22, 2023.

123. *The Kingdom, The Power, and The Glory* by Tim Alberta; P. 56; Harper Collins Publishers, 2023.

124. *Ibid.*, P. 56-57.

Falwell was a fundamentalist. He adhered to the independent Baptist code which outlawed movies, dancing, drinking, smoking, and one-on-one dating. Fundamentalism was outmoded to many young believers who were attracted to a broader, more modern Christianity concerned less with rules and more about relationships. Falwell adjusted his approach to a civic-minded, and proudly American message, one fitting to attract students to a school named Liberty University.[125]

Even after all that has been disclosed about the strategies of the Falwell ministries to blend faith with politics, I still believe the motive of Dr. Falwell was pure. He sought to influence people with his understanding of faith and his knowledge of God. But all of us build our faith on different constructs based on our experiences. Falwell's experiences led him in the direction of blending faith with politics.

THE DANGER OF FAITH AND POLITICS

The danger of combining faith with politics is evident throughout our history. The first part of this book was dedicated to illustrating the results of mixing faith with politics at an earlier time in our nation. Today, we find politics infiltrating our faith communities once again over a century after the devasting national divide called the Civil War. The blending of faith and politics has persisted over time for various reasons. Years ago, the incentive was related to the economics of an agriculturally based nation that was dependent on slave labor. Today, the incentive varies with the perspective of the participating parties. For faith leaders, it can be assumed the motive is similar to Falwell's desire to win souls and expand one's ministry for God's glory. For the politician, it is to win votes to attain and/or remain in political power.

Both politics and faith communities are ideal for blending. The initial interaction between the two is usually very provocative, inciting some response or action. This is a good business practice for both because it motivates people to act for a just cause, especially with divine implications,

---

125. *Ibid.*, P. 57.

such that, as noted by Falwell, believers should be "willing to fight" for what they believe in.

Once political considerations enter into a community of faith, however, the blending has an insidious ability to divide a body of believers. Similar to the subtle poisoning by a toxin, this blend erodes the unity of the church which is its foundation. Scripture refers to unity as being "like-minded" (Romans 15:5-6) or "living in harmony" (1 Corinthians 1:10). When politics enters the life of a faith community, neither "like-mindedness" nor "harmony" is possible because political preferences are often deemed more important than adhering to the common tenets of our faith. In other words, political preferences often trump faith issues.

For example, we may prefer a political candidate while putting aside our concern about that candidate's behavior publicly, privately, and concerning the rule of law. We may believe the greater good comes from supporting such a candidate who will deliver on an issue that aligns with our particular faith regardless of the conflicts in our faith supporting that candidate. That is the exact calculation Falwell made when he politically supported Ronald Reagan and aligned against Jimmy Carter. These efforts may be successful initially, but eventually they will divide the universal community of faith.

Decisions made in our faith communities that are based on political preferences have long-term consequences that sometimes are not realized until decades later. These decisions sow discord in our faith communities and confusion in our nation at large. Discord within the faith communities because not all people have the same beliefs or doctrines guiding their faith. Confusion in our nation at large because Christians appear hypocritical and compromised at times, which undermines any message of faith we desire to project. Scripture clearly states God is not the author of confusion (1 Corinthians 14:33). So, we can assume that any actions that confuse the communities of faith are not ordained by God but rather result from man's own devices. Neither political party is immune from this behavior. "Evangelicals" are both Republicans and Democrats.

Winston Churchill is credited with saying, "Those who fail to learn from history are doomed to repeat it." To learn from history, one must first understand the facts and then the context of the events. Faith is polluted by politics because neither the facts nor the context is understood by a large segment of "evangelicals," based on my experience of many years in that community of faith. Once in the church, we tend to believe we are on sacred ground, and we inherently trust those who lead and disciple us. Many of us are ignorant of the subtleties of current events. If our spiritual leaders declare something by the authority and in the name of God, we trust them and accept what is declared. It is only natural for a faith community to act in faith, but we often do not know the construct of our leader's faith.

For example, I sat under Jerry Falwell's tutelage many times, but I did not know the construct of his faith until recently. I didn't know enough about the constitution of our nation to recognize when a preacher was advocating against its principles. I didn't know enough about the history of our nation and the devasting effects of blending faith with politics.

When a renowned journalist takes four years out of his life to investigate the faith community he has known all his life, the faith that his father dedicated his life to serving, and declares it to be "deteriorating," something is seriously wrong. The fact is we, the people of faith, are all complicit when an entire nation is headed in the wrong direction as we seem to be doing.

The evidence of that complicity is all over the world. To illustrate the pervasiveness of this complicity, let's consider the example of Russia presented by Alberta. Russia is very relevant in the current dynamic of world events and specifically relevant as an example of the blending of faith and politics in a nation today.

FAITH AND POLITICS IN RUSSIA

I can remember sitting in class as a child in Catholic grammar school and learning about the Communist threat to our nation that existed in Russia at that time. We were taught that Russia's state religion was atheism and they believed that there was no God. Evidently, what we were taught was part of the 1958-1964 anti-religion campaign of Nikita Khrushchev, Secretary of the Communist Party at that time.

That is not the case today in Russia. The national faith in Russia today is (Orthodox) Christianity and has been for over 1000 years, since the baptism of Olga in the 950s to the baptism of her grandson Vladimir in 988 (often, and disputably, considered the birth date of Christianity in Russia—at the time, Kyivan Russia). With the advent of Marxism-Leninism, the practice of Christianity went underground, often with severe repercussions for those practicing their faith, reappearing only after *raspad* (the dissolution of the Soviet Union in December 1991). However, only a fraction of the Russian people today is practicing Christians. For the vast majority—an estimated 80% of the country's citizens—Christianity is cultural. The distinction being made between practicing and cultural speaks to a difference in the formality of their faith. Practicing Russian Christians incorporate more of a formal function and routine as a critical part of their faith. In other words, they routinely go to church. Cultural Russian Christians refer to their faith as an identity, which usually means a more casual practice of their faith. For the majority of Russian Christians, their faith is not defined by doctrine but takes root as a form of nationalism. "Orthodox Christian nationalism has been on the rise in Russia from the collapse of the Soviet Union, the by-product of a state desperate to rediscover legitimacy in the eyes of a chastened and aimless populace." [126]

From my college days up until age 30 I identified myself as a Catholic, but I stopped any practical practice of my Catholic faith. At that time, I could have been characterized as a cultural Catholic. It has been my experience that many in our nation are cultural Christians, cultural Jews, and members of many other cultural faiths as well. So, the Russian experience of having cultural Christians is not unique, and the experience is common within our own nation.

Additionally, in our country Christian faith communities are divided by doctrine (i.e., Pentecostal, non-Pentecostal, Catholic,

---

126. *Ibid.*, P. 233.

Baptist, Lutheran, etc.) Likewise in Russia, Christianity is divided into denominations as well. The largest is the Russian Orthodox Church, a branch of Eastern Orthodoxy, with 170 different dioceses. The number of Catholics is estimated to be from 600,000 to 1.5 million. There are over 1 million Protestants, as well as smaller representations of other religions: Islam and Judaism, for example.[127] Since *raspad*, missionaries from several Christian denominations, including the Church of the Latter-Day Saints, have actively attempted to evangelize some of the more remote parts of Russia. However, today, after the beginning of the war in Ukraine, such activities have become dangerous, at least for Westerners, and significantly curtailed.

In our nation, Christian churches are divided by race as well within those common denominations. There are multi-racial Christian churches (my wife and I are currently attending one in a Maryland suburb not far from Washington D.C.). For the most part Black, Hispanic, and Asian churches are separate bodies of believers. It is said that Sunday morning is one of the most segregated times in our nation. There is no such racial division in the Russian Orthodox Church; however, in the former Soviet republics, most attendees at Orthodox services will reflect the local ethnic community (e.g., Georgians, Armenians, and the like).

In 2007, Vladimir Putin announced at a global security forum his desire to recreate the Old Soviet empire. He began to create a spiritual rationale for policies that might otherwise prove unpopular. In 2014, Russia invaded and annexed the Ukraine territory of Crimea, a blatant violation of international law. This violation of law along with the bloody campaign that followed was made palatable to the Russian people thanks to Moscow's rhetoric of divine destiny.

By the time of Ukraine's 2022 invasion, Putin's propaganda had been perfected to cast it in terms of religious obligation. His message was given credibility with the spiritual cover of the religious leaders, Kiril and All Rus. Dating from the days of the tsars, except during the time of the USSR, church and state have been intertwined. This made it easy

---

127. Wikipedia, "Christianity in Russia"

to convince the Russian people that they were fighting "a sacred war" to liberate Ukraine. Russian troops were assured their fight was against secularists, apostates, and even Nazis. If they were to lay down their life for their country, they would be with God. This was described as the political theology of Putinism.

The war in Ukraine has not met Putin's expectations. The Ukrainians defended their country with heart, soul, and everything they had—ably. Experiencing this, many Russian troops lost heart; their morale dissipated. The religious exhortations of the faraway faded over the distance. Some felt deceived when they did not find apostates or Nazis in Ukraine, but Ukrainian soldiers and citizens that they would have called friends, brother Slavs, and even relatives in the not-distant past, who were clearly neither in need of nor desirous for liberation.

Regardless of the crumbling morale of the Russian troops, the propaganda campaign was still highly effective back home. "With the aid of state-run media and a blockade against Western information, the Kremlin had convinced much of the Russian public that their sons were engaged in a sanctified struggle."[128]

When people senses that God has a special mission for them, they often do not feel constrained by moral norms but assume the mission allows them the freedom to do whatever they believe needs to be done. Alberta describes Putin not as a religious man but a leader who practices "an eclectic theology" that cherry-picks whatever spiritual concepts support his ideological agenda. The one thing Putin believes in is power. By weaponizing religion, Putin had accumulated more power than ever before. "Russia wasn't merely using Christianity to endorse its ambitions. Russia was using Christianity to define its enemies. That would not have been possible without the blessing of the Russian Church."[129]

(On a side note, the patriarch and the president do not always agree, except in public, but they have respect for each other as can be seen in public gatherings. A little-known fact is that Putin was baptized during

---

128. *Ibid.*, P. 235.

129. *Ibid*, P.235-236

Soviet times—by the father of the present-day patriarch.[130] As with much of everything in Russia, the seemingly obvious can turn out to be complicated.)

Over my lifetime, Russia has transitioned from a nation trying to eliminate religion to one that has integrated a nationalistic faith into its political strategy. The success of this strategy requires two critical elements. First, a cooperation of the nation's faith-based leaders with the political powers and second a general population that views its faith as cultural and is willing to follow national faith leaders. Those methods have been effective in Russia. Those same strategies have been effective in our nation over recent presidential elections. Specifically, the blending of faith with politics has been embraced first through a cooperative effort by the faith community leaders and then a winning over of the faith communities through a controlled media message. Let's look at how this Russian model has been employed in our nation.

RUSSIAN MODEL: COOPERATION OF "EVANGELICAL LEADERS"

I was appalled by President Bill Clinton's sexual indiscretions in the White House in 1998. I was deeply upset when Democrats in the Senate refused to remove him from office after his impeachment. I was deeply involved in my career and ministry in the evangelical church at the time and did not take the time to follow all the details. All I knew from my many years of Civil Service was that if any other Federal Employee had been involved in something similar to that of President Clinton, he or she would no longer be allowed to continue in their Federal Service. To see the President of the United States continue in his job without consequence was an insult to every Federal Civil Servant. I believe that event introduced to our country a tolerance for unruly behavior in the Oval Office going forward. The boundaries for acceptable behavior of

---

130. "Russian Orthodoxy and Politics in the Putin Era" By Gregory Freeze. *Task Force on U.S. Policy Toward Russia, Ukraine, and Eurasia*. Carnegie Endowment for International Peace, 2017.

a president had been changed at that point. We had no idea how much presidential behaviors would change shortly.

Up until Clinton's successful evasion of political punishment (or at least fall out) from scandal, the religious right had expected chaste behavior from public officials and made it clear that Clinton's womanizing made him unfit to be president. Godly character was needed—and he did not have it, according to the declarations of the religious right. That all changed with Donald Trump.

When Donald Trump secured the 2016 GOP presidential nomination, there was justifiable alarm among many Christians. Trump had spent his campaign inciting hatred against his critics, hurling vicious ad hominem insults at his opponents, boasting of his never having asked God's forgiveness, and generally behaving in ways that were antithetical to the example of Christ. Trump gave no evidence of what Scripture calls "the fruit of the spirit," that is, those characteristics such as love, peace, joy, gentleness, self-control, grace, humility, and others that mark the life of a person of faith. (Galatians 5:22,23) Trump's allies among the leaders of evangelical Christians knew they had to address this issue for the GOP nominee to make it to the White House.

Evangelical leaders then deployed a novel strategy to ignore the sins of Trump's behavior: they embraced his shortcomings. Franklin Graham, Mike Huckabee, and other Trump allies began to refer to him as the latest in a long tradition of flawed men who were being used by God to advance His purposes; the scriptures were filled with examples of such leaders Trump thus was sanctioned by the evangelical leaders of the day and released into the politico-sphere with their blessing. This support licensed Trump to endorse all the religious rhetoric he desired to cajole, charm, and lie to an evangelical base waiting to embrace him. The religious tactic used by Trump were similar to those used by Putin on the other side of the world: winning over a base of evangelical support. It was a relatively simple task with already having the support of key evangelical leaders.

Trump had campaigned in 2016 on the promise that "Christianity will have power" if he won the White House. In 2020 he warned that his opponent Joe Biden was going to "hurt God" and target Christians for their religious beliefs. His campaign resorted to threats, dark rhetoric, innuendos of violence (if not actual violence), conspiracy theories, and prophesied apocalypse. Evangelical leaders painted a picture of spiritual warfare between the God-fearing Republicans who supported Trump and secular Democrats, who viewed Trump as an obstacle to overcoming America's Judeo-Christian ethos.

This parallels the tone and context of the message used by Putin in equating his political takeover of Ukraine. In describing his military action as a spiritual battle, the Russian army represented the good force, and the Ukraine represented the evil to be destroyed. My wife had a recent experience to illustrate how effective this technique is when applied to politics in our nation. In a bible study my wife was attending, one lady referred to our current president as "evil Biden." It is a very effective method for evangelicals to accept a political preference if it is a simple choice of good versus evil. The accuracy of the message, however, doesn't matter to most who use that type of messaging.

Throughout Trump's administration, select evangelical leaders continued to support him. I referenced earlier the anecdotal case of Rusell Moore, a leader in his evangelical denomination. To hold a leadership position in his denomination, absolute fealty to Trump was required. Moore's decision not to support President Trump was the cause of his fall from grace and loss of leadership position. Moore's and Alberta's writings provide ample anecdotal evidence to illustrate that the committed loyalty of evangelical leaders to Trump prompted congregants to follow.

RUSSIAN MODEL: WINNING OVER THE FAITH COMMUNITIES

Tucker Carlson, at a time when he was still the top-rated Fox News personality, spent the first year of the Ukraine War defending Putin's honor. Carlson, while downplaying Putin's savagery, described America's aid to Ukraine as a secular "jihad" aimed at toppling "an orthodox Christian country with traditional values." He was joined in this effort by Congresswoman Marjorie Taylor Greene who ranted about "the war against Russia in Ukraine," as opposed to the reality, the war against Ukraine by Russia. Carlson's programming was played in a loop on Russian state television to reinforce the Kremlin's talking points.[131]

We do not have a state-run communication system in our nation that broadcasts the desired political message of an authoritarian ruler, but we have something close to it. In the pursuit of freedom of speech and the free enterprise system, we have communication systems over various mediums commercially available that are dedicated to focusing on and selectively biased toward a desired political outcome-based message. We can select the political message of our choice that is made available to us 24 hours a day, seven days a week, and 52 weeks a year over the medium of our choice. That exceeds the capability of any existing autocratic state-run broadcast by far.

The nature of this political news business in our nation has grown so large and so powerful that stories can be told without regard to their validity or accuracy until a network or the individual perpetrator is stopped through a lawsuit. Recent court cases represent the continued lying and spreading of false information that relentlessly occurs until stopped by litigation.

Fox News agreed to pay Dominion Voting Systems $787.5 million and acknowledged the court's earlier ruling that Fox had broadcast false statements about Dominion's accuracy during the last presidential election. The settlement did not require Fox News to apologize. It is the largest known media settlement for defamation in U.S. history. Other similar lawsuits are pending.

The families of Sandy Hook shooting victims offered Infowars host Alex Jones a way to avoid bankruptcy if he paid them a small portion of the more than $1 billion he owed in damages, according to a court document. Jones filed for personal bankruptcy in December 2022 after he was ordered to pay the damages when he lost two civil cases over his false claims about the elementary school massacre. Rudy Guliani was ordered to pay two Geogia election workers $148 million for defaming them.

---

131. *Ibid.*, P. 235.

With this barrage of false information supported by the most popular news channels, it is easy to disseminate a false narrative. If that false narrative is supported by the leaders of a faith community, it is easy to persuade a faith gathering, a faith congregation, a faith denomination, and a majority of evangelicals today. I do not think it is any more complex than that because that was my personal experience for many years.

In our fast-paced society, we resort to news sound bites as we go on our daily routine to satisfy the minimum requirement we need to "sound informed" if the situation presents itself. There is no time for deep analysis. A quick check is all that is needed to either dismiss or embrace the latest news flash depending on whether it fits into our current construct established by our preferred blend of politics and faith. Quite often we are left with a political narrative that is no more accurate than if we got our information by surfing Tic Tok or from a glance of a tabloid headline as we pass by a newsstand on the street or in a store.

Evangelicals for the most part do not invest a lot of time in researching political issues or political candidates. Often additional demands on their time are experienced through commitments to church services or ministry involvement as part of their faith experience. Most do a quick check on issues to see that they align with their doctrinal beliefs and/or glean what they can from their denominational leaders. That is why evangelical leaders many years ago politicized the abortion issue. It acts as a quick litmus test to decide how to vote and whom to support politically. It doesn't require any more thought than that, and it was exactly what I did for many years. That is the custom of the evangelicals I know today, and I believe many others as well. Consequently, many evangelicals simply are being led into the fold as sheep by their shepherds. It is quite different from the example in scripture where Christ says, "My sheep hear My voice, and I know them, and they follow Me" (John 10:27). Christ's admonition is to listen for and to hear "His voice". What most are doing are listening to voices that declare they are "hearing from God" for us. I believe God has the ability and desire to speak to us individually. We do not need an interpreter for God if we are listening for His voice directly.

CHARACTERIZING "EVANGELICALS" TODAY

Ryan P. Burge is an assistant professor of political science at Eastern Illinois University. He is also a pastor in the American Baptist Church, having served his congregation for more than fifteen years. Burge states that the best way to measure the size of evangelicalism over time is through self-identification. Past surveys relied on identifying evangelicals by the denomination to which they belonged. However, many surveys have begun to include an additional question about religious identification: "Do you consider yourself to be a born-again or evangelical Christian, or not?" The person hearing the question determines their religious attachment. This process is called "self-identification."[132]

I agree Burge's assessment is correct if you are trying to identify the subtleties of an individual's faith. In other words, these are correct questions if we want to know the doctrinal differences or other distinctions that separate evangelical from other Christians. These are often similar to the techniques used when trying to identify evangelicals as part of an election analysis.

If we are trying to understand the political allegiances of evangelicals today, that is not the right question. The correct question to ask is "How does a person reconcile their politics with their faith?" Or more specifically, "How can people whose faith is vitally important to them support a political candidate who conflicts with their faith in so many areas?"

The answer to those questions refers back to our initial discussion in this chapter concerning the construct of our faith. The faith experience is a continuum of experiences. It is a growing, changing dynamic that if left static will become stale and routine. Unless our faith becomes revitalized, it will wither to the extent it can be difficult to determine if it still lives within us or not. At best, it is vibrant, changing, and

132. *20 Myths about Religion and Politics in America* by Ryan P. Burge; P.15; Fortress Press, 2022.

transformative. Operating in this way, our faith offers a dimension to life that is unmatched by anything else we do. Which trajectory our faith journey follows, static or vibrant, depends largely on our mentoring, our shepherding in the local body of believers, and the desires of the individual heart. Most, if not all, are good, sincere people seeking a relationship with God that they can understand and a fellowship of like-minded believers who can be embraced as a part of their spiritual identity.

The construct of faith that seems to best characterize a contemporary evangelical cannot be constrained by denomination, doctrine, or an exact form or function of faith. It cannot be characterized as Pentecostal or non-Pentecostal. It cannot be labeled as non-denominational or independent. The evangelical today is a blend of patriotism and religion. Christian nationalism is more often the norm for the present-day evangelical than not, with some not even being familiar with the term. The evangelicals of today perceive that they are in a battle of good versus evil. Good being the like-minded, evil being all others. Compromise is a bad word. A willingness to fight is good because they are in an epic battle for the ages. The evangelical of today, when faced with a choice between politics and faith, will defer to politics in pursuit of the greater good as they understand it.

The problem with this type of characterization is that it conflicts with the standard ways of identifying an evangelical today. Additionally, I have noticed some political polls identify evangelicals simply by their high frequency of church attendance with no other distinction. Alberta has a different perspective:

> The crisis of American evangelicalism comes down to an obsession with that worldly identity. Instead of fixing our eyes on the unseen, "since what is seen is temporary, but what is unseen is eternal," as Paul writes in Second Corinthians, we have become fixated on the here and now.[133]

---

133. *The Kingdom, The Power, and The Glory* by Tim Alberta; P. 13; Harper Collins Publishers, 2023.

I cannot argue with that view. It offers a better explanation for the current evangelical phenomenon than I can offer. We find ourselves in a precarious place. Our faith identities are being confused by the blending of faith and politics. We all know how difficult it is to identify anything once it spends enough time in a blender. The more elements that are thrown into the mix the harder it is to identify what we have as a result.

Our current blend combines a polarized political message with a variety of different faith communities. To make it more difficult, these faith communities with different denominational beliefs are often sprinkled with racial undertones inherited from the history of our nation. It is no wonder we have difficulty in identifying who we are. One may characterize the evangelical of today as being in an identity crisis. The challenge now is how we go forward as a united nation in this blended concoction of faith we find ourselves.

SOME FINAL THOUGHTS

The vision of the universal Christian church as described in scripture is as one body. Over the years, that universal body has been divided into denominational differences accommodating each believer's measure and preference of faith. But even with those denominational differences, in the past there existed an overall harmony of faith. It was easy to celebrate a common core of beliefs that we could still define as one faith. We are in a different season now. The divide created by the blending of faith and politics has dispersed us to opposite corners of the ring, and we are like two boxers poised to lunge at one another at the sound of the bell introducing the next round of fighting. Once the bell sounds each is determined to bring the other down. Ding, ding, ding ..... fighting over gun rights. Ding, ding, ding .... fighting over abortion rights. Ding, ding, ding .... fighting over the next presidential election. Once that bell sounds announcing the subject of the round, we start sparring with one another trying to identify our opponent's vulnerability. Once an opening is identified we maneuver close trying to land the first punch. Once the fight begins, unless common decency prevails, it can get very bloody. Wounds are opened up that do not quickly heal. Relationships take on a new form, one that neither party cares to continue. Then, the division takes root, and the relationship is severed. I have been in too many of those fights. We have to do better.

The final few chapters of this book will propose a method of removing the gloves, climbing out of the ring, pulling up a chair, and working through this blended mess together. The goal is to begin to establish unity in the faith communities of our nation first. Then, we can move on together uniting our country.

CHAPTER 12

A Common Identity

On a hot August day in the summer of 1968, my parents drove me to Lexington, Virginia to matriculate into the Virginia Military Institute's class of 1972. We arrived at the school mid-morning after having driven down from New Jersey the day before and spending the night at a local hotel. We took our time with a leisurely breakfast because it was my first experience of leaving home for an extended period and we were in no hurry to end our time together. My parents were not planning to return to Lexington until Parent's Weekend scheduled for some time in the fall. At that moment, their revisit seemed like an eternity away.

It first occurred to me that I was entering a new life experience when my parents and I were quickly separated on our arrival on campus that morning. We were directed to drop off my bags in the designated area and to say our goodbyes. My parents would not be allowed to escort me through the registration process but were assured I would be in good hands. The process itself was simple and well-organized. I was welcomed each step of the way by a smiling upperclassman or an administrator. It wasn't until an hour or so later that I left the administrative area and crossed the street into the cadet barracks. There "all hell broke loose!"

As we entered the barracks area, we were greeted by a cadre of upperclassmen specifically selected to instruct us in the "VMI tradition" of first-year students referred to as the "rat line." All freshmen were "rats," and our classmates were designated as our "brother rats." At that point, our heads were shaved, our civilian clothes were stored away, and our instruction of life as a "rat" began. This intense orientation would last several weeks until the remainder of the student body returned for the new academic year. These initial days were long, hot, and filled with physical exercise and military training from early morning to late night. There was order and conformity introduced into every aspect of our new life, starting with the way we made our beds, folded our underwear, tucked our shirts, and learned to march in a synchronized movement.

Once the academic year began, our daily routine was filled with classes, military duties, intermural athletics, and a lot of study time. We traveled in formation to meals, classes, and even to church on Sundays. We were always striving to appear and function as a singular unit, mindful of each other, and always willing to help our "brother rat" if needed. Through that process, we forged relationships that have lasted a lifetime.

As crude and barbaric as that way of life sounds, it was an effective way to achieve the desired outcome. The desired outcome was to mold a body of over 300 young men from all over the nation and two foreign countries into a cohesive, unified body. That process involved having hundreds of individual identities adopt a single common identity and training young men of different skills, talents, interests, and experiences to put aside personal preferences to focus on conducting ourselves as a single-minded military unit. This is a common core practice embraced by all the military services in our nation. One body, united by a common identity, dedicated to one common purpose. That common purpose is to preserve, protect, and defend our nation when called to do so.

A similar phenomenon occurs when we enter into our faith journey. Although there are many faiths, I find there is a commonality in the faith experience of three of the major faiths of this world. This commonality of faith experience is what I refer to as a common faith identity. This common faith identity can be a source of unity and acceptance of one another, despite the differences in each faith, similar to the experience of forming a military body united by a common purpose.

COMMON IDENTITY: JUDAISM, ISLAM, CHRISTIANITY

The book of Genesis describes the origin of a common heritage of the Jewish, Islamic, and Christian faiths. The 17th chapter captures a covenant made between God and a man named Abram, renamed by God as Abraham. The covenant was initially described simply as God promising Abraham that he would "multiply exceedingly." Later on, after Abraham passed the test of faith by willingly offering his only son Isaac as a sacrifice to God (was an offering stopped by God at the last moment), the covenant was expounded on by God. "By Myself I have sworn, says the Lord, because you have done this thing, and have not withheld your son, in blessing I will bless you, and in multiplying I will multiply your descendants as the stars of the heaven and as the sand which is on the seashore; and your descendants shall possess the gates of their enemies. In your seed all the nations of the earth shall be blessed, because you have obeyed my voice" (Genesis 22:16-18).

Looking at the natural lineage of this man called Abraham, we find he had several children but the two of primary concern for our purpose are Ishmael and Isaac. Ishmael's lineage can be traced to the prophet Muhammed and Islam. Isaac's lineage can be traced to the 12 tribes of Israel and the Jewish nation as well as to Jesus Christ and the Christian church. That is a whole lot of folks when you combine the lineage of both sons. If the prophecy was a metaphor for the spiritual heritage of the three forms of faith (Judaism, Islam, and Christianity) then we are dealing with a countless number of souls involved.

Of course, there are vast differences in the doctrines of belief between the faiths of Christianity and Judaism, and even more so when considering Islam, but one could make the argument that if all three faiths descend from the same God there must be some commonality in the spiritual makeup of these three faiths, a common gene in the spiritual DNA of each faith to use a medical metaphor. I have witnessed similar characteristics in people of all three of these faiths. I had Muslim students when I taught high school math who were humble, kind, and respectful in class even when surrounded by a peer group of unruly students. I have worked with Jewish associates in government and private business who had qualities in their demeanor that were similar to those attributes described in scripture as products of faith. I observed attributes such as humility, peace, joy, patience, kindness, goodness, and self-control that we as Christians believe are gifts from God (Galatians 5:22) in people of both Jewish and Muslim faiths.

Scripture traces the common lineage of these three faiths (Judaism, Islam, and Christianity) back to the same God we Christians believe to be the one true God. If so, it makes sense that these same attributes would exist in people whose origin of faith is in the same God. I would suggest these common products of faith from our common God are the spiritual DNA that I referred to previously. This is faith's common identity. That is, a person of faith is peaceful, kind, thinking of others more than themselves, devout, and humble before the God of their understanding. This is the identity that resides in the soul of each person of faith—Christian, Jew, and Muslim.

However, when looking at diverse faiths like the three mentioned, it is difficult to recognize any commonality. The reason is we tend to focus on the obvious external differences of each faith and very seldom look for any commonality, particularly in what comes out of those faiths. It becomes even more challenging to identify the commonalities within different Christian denominations because of the wide diversity in doctrines and practices. When we look at denominations outside our own preferred form of Christian faith, we often focus on the differences rather than the common attributes.

DENOMINATIONAL DIVERSITY OF CHRISTIANITY

The common identity of faith becomes more difficult to identify, given the added organizational layers of denominations. Google tells us there are 27 Christian denominations in the United States. The top five are Catholicism, Protestantism, Anglicanism, Eastern Orthodoxy, and Oriental Orthodoxy. In addition, there are approximately 100 protestant denominations in the United States with the five largest being the Southern Baptist Convention, United Methodist Church, National Baptist Convention, Evangelical Lutheran Church, and Assemblies of God.

While it is difficult to characterize this diverse a denominational list, there seems to be a consensus among two major groups of denominations. The Southern Baptist Convention embodies the first group known as the evangelical movement. The second group, known as mainline protestants, is represented by the United Methodist Church. Mainline protestants are less conservative than evangelicals. For example, mainline denominations allow women to be pastors and are open and affirming to LGBT individuals, contrary to the evangelical movement which has strict boundaries in both areas.[134] Many denominations have struggled to keep their denominational identity while accommodating the increased demand for social diversity.

Incorporating diversity in mainline protestant denominations has affected denominations in differing ways. The Episcopal Church pursued a more liberal Christian course in the 1960s and 1970s. In 2007-2008, four dioceses of the Episcopal Church voted to join the Anglican Church of the Southern Cone of America. In December 2008, 12 other jurisdictions of the Episcopal Church, serving an estimated 100,000 persons at that time, formed the Anglican Church in North America (ACNA).[135] The Presbyterian Church in the United States of America (PCUSA), formed in 1789, currently exists in two denominations. The Presbyterian Church in America (PCA) is the largest conservative Calvinist denomination. The Presbyterian Church (USA) voted to allow same-sex marriages in 2014, making it one of the largest Christian denominations to accept same-sex unions.[136]

---

134. *20 Myths about Religion and Politics in America* by Ryan P. Burge, P. 65; Fortress Press, 2022.

135. Wikipedia; "Episcopal Church (United States)"

136. Wikipedia; "The Presbyterian Church in the United States"

Other examples of diversity include the Lutheran Church and the United Methodist Church. Both illustrate differences within their denominations. In the first example, the Evangelical Lutheran Church of America (ECLA) allows the ordination of women, while the Lutheran Church–Missouri Synod (LCMS), which is the second-largest Lutheran body in the United States after the ECLA, does not ordain women. The second example is the United Methodist Church with an estimated 10.4 million members, which has current policies that are strongly against the LGBTQ community. However, many of the church leaders, including local pastors, welcome gays and lesbians as church members and support their basic human rights.[137] These are examples of churches trying to hold on to their denominational identities while accommodating a diverse membership body.

We cannot conclude our discussion about diversity in the Christian Church without looking at the various positions concerning abortion. This issue has proven to be one of our nation's most divisive social issues. The diverse denominational positions on abortion illustrate that many Christians have different beliefs on this subject. The following are a few examples courtesy of a report by the Pew Research Center, dated January 16, 2013, titled "Religious Groups' Official Positions on Abortion."

- *The American Baptist Churches in the U.S.A.* recognize the different views on abortion among its members and its General Board encourages women and couples "to seek spiritual counsel as they prayerfully consider their decision." Though the board opposes abortion "as a primary means of birth control," it does not condemn abortion outright.

- *The Evangelical Lutheran Church in America* official position states that "abortion before viability [of a fetus] should not be prohibited by law or by lack of public funding" but that abortion after the point of fetal viability should be prohibited except when

---

137. Wikipedia;" The Lutheran Church" and "The United Methodist Church".

the life of a mother is threatened or when fetal abnormalities pose a fatal threat to the newborn.

- *The Lutheran Church-Missouri Synod* states that "since abortion takes a human life, it is not a moral option except to prevent the death of the mother."

- *The National Association of Evangelicals* has passed many resolutions stating its opposition to abortion. However, the organization recognizes that there might be situations in which terminating a pregnancy is warranted – such as protecting the life of a mother or in cases of rape or incest.

- *The National Council of Churches* does not have an official position on abortion because of the diverse theological teachings of its member churches.

- *The Presbyterian Church (U.S.A.)* General Assembly reaffirmed its belief in 2006 that the termination of a pregnancy is a personal decision. While the church disapproves of abortion as a means of birth control or as a method of convenience, it seeks "to maintain within its fellowship those who, based on a study of Scripture and prayerful decision, come to diverse conclusions and actions" on the issue.

- *The Southern Baptist Convention* in a 1996 resolution on partial-birth abortion reaffirmed its opposition to abortion, stating that "all human life is a sacred gift from God and therefore …. all abortions, except in those very rare cases where the life of the mother is clearly in danger, are wrong."

- *The United Church of Christ* is a firm advocate of reproductive rights, including the right to a safe abortion.

- *The United Methodist Church* while opposing abortion, affirms that it is "equally bound to respect the sacredness of the life and well-being of the mother and the unborn child." The church sanctions "the legal option of abortion under medical procedures" but rejects abortion as a method of gender selection or birth control and stresses that those considering abortions should prayerfully seek guidance from their doctors, families, and ministers.

It should be noted as we conclude this discussion on abortion, that none of the listed Protestant denominations, including both mainline and evangelical denominations, embraces the total elimination of abortion. Even the most stringent positions allow for special exceptions concerning the life of the mother or fetus or both. The fact that several states are currently advocating for a total ban on abortion and the criminalization of the act when it occurs illustrates the politicization of this issue that has been directed at the evangelical Christian community. That is, because of political influence, many evangelical Christians are advocating positions on abortion that exceed most Christian denominational standards.

The point of this discussion on the diversity of Christianity is to illustrate the wide range of positions on various social issues. The Christian Church exercises no common approach. However, my faith journey has included multiple protestant denominations, and it was my experience that each denomination believes they are interpreting scripture and the mandates of their faith correctly. When denominations differ in their interpretation of scripture or have different denominational mandates, judgments are usually made, and labels are sometimes assigned such as "liberal" or "conservative." Often, explanations are offered that those people are "deceived" or "not really Christians." What is being implied is that those that believe differently are not Christians like us.

Regardless of the side of the argument, each denomination defends its position based on scripture, sometimes opposite arguments from the same scriptural reference. For example, 1 Corinthians Chapter 13 is used as a scriptural reference both to justify the gift of tongues as existing today and to justify the claim that it is now extinct. My point is not to criticize any person's faith or any denominational position but simply to illustrate that our common Christian identity must transcend our denominational differences. In other words, our common identity as a Christian must be defined outside our denominational definitions.

So, what is the common Christian identity that all Christian denominations can use? What is it that bonds us together in faith instead of dividing us over our denominational differences? Let's look at scripture and what it says about the common identity of the Christian faith.

CHRISTIANITY'S COMMON IDENTITY

Many characteristics can be assigned to the people of the Christian faith in scripture. However, the single most distinctive feature assigned to the people of God that is consistent in both the Old Testament and the New Testament writings is "unity." Unity is defined as "oneness," the quality or state of not being multiple. Unity in the people of faith is the setting aside of all our individualism and acting in accord with one another for some divine purpose.

David was an Old Testament shepherd, psalmist, soldier, leader of armies, and king who was described as "a man after God's own heart" (1 Samuel 13:14). David was a man of worship who literally danced before God (2 Samuel 6:14). David writes "Behold, how good and how pleasant it is for brethren to dwell together in unity" (Psalm 133:1). He goes on to use a metaphor in that psalm comparing that unity of the people of faith to the anointing oil that was poured over the head, beard, and garments of the high priest Aaron as he prepared to enter the tabernacle of the temple where the presence of God was dwelling. In other words, unity prepares the people of God for the presence of God in their lives. When the people of faith are unified, they have come together as one single identity through which God can manifest His will and His purposes. Without unity, the body of believers is disjointed and ineffective in achieving God's purposes for our lives.

The Apostle Paul describes the unity of the people of God in the New Testament in a different way. Writing to the people of faith in Ephesus, he refers to "the unity of the Spirit in the bond of peace." He goes on to describe this unity as "one Lord, one faith, one baptism, one God and Father of all, who is above all, and through all, and in you all" (Ephesians 4:3-6). That is, we are all *united* in our common faith that comes from our one God and is in all of us. He starts this description with the words "I beseech you" and "endeavoring." In other words, Paul is saying "I beg you to work at keeping" this unity that God has placed in the people of God through faith.

The apostle Paul knew that unity did not come easy to people of faith, particularly the first-century Christian Church. Most of Paul's epistles address the lack of unity and discord that existed in the young church during his ministry. Things have become decidedly more difficult and complex over the 2,000 years that have passed since Paul's writings. It is no surprise that we have such difficulty in pursuing unity in the church today.

Paul knew of the diversity in the church. In his writing to the church at Corinth, he says "Now there are diversities of gifts, but the same Spirit. There are differences of ministries, but the same Lord. And there are diversities of activities, but it is the same God who works all in all" (1 Corinthians 12:4-6). We are all different creations of God. We are different in our gifts and our talents. We see things differently from one another. That is a strength, not a weakness. Paul explains it as follows. "But to each one of us grace was given according to the measure of Christ's gift" (Ephesians 4:7). It is only God's grace that can make all this work. Our challenge is to let God's grace work in each of our lives. Let me explain.

The identity of the Christian Church should be its unity because it is only by God's grace, His unmerited favor toward us, that we can be unified despite all our diversity. We do not have to give up our doctrinal and denominational beliefs to be unified. We have so much common ground in our Christian faith that we can be united in those areas. We can agree to disagree on those other areas of faith that divide us into our denominational silos.

How do we do that? The author of the Book of Hebrews states "… let us lay aside every weight, and the sin which so easily ensnares us, and let us run with endurance the race that is set before us …" (Hebrews 12:1). Sin? What sin? How can it be a sin to live our faith in the way we believe is scripturally sound and sanctioned by those who lead our respective denomination? The answer is *that is not the sin* that entangles us and destroys our unity with others who believe differently from us. The sin that stops our unity is our pride and refusal to humble ourselves to one another.

The apostle Peter addressed a problem of division in the early church between the elders and the younger people. His advice was "All of you be submissive to one another and be clothed in humility for God resists the proud but gives grace to the humble" (I Peter 5:5). It doesn't matter who we think is right or who we think is wrong. It doesn't matter who is more mature in their faith and who is less mature in their faith. What matters is that we humble ourselves for the sake of unity of faith. We are to humble ourselves with one another. If not, we are fighting ourselves and God is resisting us as well. If we are to believe Peter's counsel, God is literally making our way difficult when we act out in pride. Unfortunately, I can testify to that fact from my personal experience. The quicker we learn to "let go and let God," the less frustrated we will be. Once we do that, we still face some severe challenges to achieve a common Christian identity of unity. Let me describe three of them.

CHRISTIANITY'S COMMON IDENTITY FIRST CHALLENGE: DENOMINATIONS

I have chronicled in detail my faith journey from being raised Catholic to eventually being a licensed and ordained minister in the International Pentecostal Holiness Church (IPHC) in my first writing *The Evidence of Things Unseen*. My transition from Catholic to Protestant faith began with an independent Baptist church. That church was pastored by a young man, several years younger than I, who became not only my pastor but also a good friend. Everything he taught and preached was based on his understanding of scripture, which was rooted in his Baptist training. He was adamant in his convictions and was a convincing advocate for me to believe likewise.

One of the denominational positions taught at that time pertained to the gifts of the Holy Spirit (1 Corinthians 12:8-10). It was taught that those gifts were active in the first-century church but no longer appropriate today. Although nine gifts are listed in scripture, the one emphasized the most was that of speaking in tongues. This practice was considered a threat to the universal church because it was believed to be a tool used to usher in the "end times" depicted in the Book of Revelation. Of course, this was my pastor's opinion, formulated through his denominational experience and such an account does not appear anywhere in scripture. This position was part of the initial teaching of my newfound faith and prejudiced my view of faith going forward. Years later, my position on these gifts of the Holy Spirit changed when God brought me into the Pentecostal faith experience.[138]

Approximately 25 years later I returned for a visit to that same Baptist church. My friend was still pastoring, and it was a rewarding time of renewed relationship. One visit turned out to be several with many discussions catching up with all the events in both our families over the years. He knew I had become Pentecostal and volunteered that he had changed his position on that whole experience. He had become close friends with a Pentecostal pastor and learned to accept his ministry. He still believed that being Pentecostal was not for him but had no problem having a fellowship of faith with Pentecostals. This lifelong Baptist pastor even jointly participated in a few Pentecostal services.

Two pastors from different denominations humbled themselves from their denominational differences and discovered a common identity of faith. In that act, a unity was created that crossed denominations. That experience with my pastor friend affected not only the relationship between us two pastors but also each our pastoral relationships with others. A case in point was the newfound respect between my pastor of many years ago and me. We now see ourselves as brothers in the faith again as we did many years ago. Like the apostle Paul said, "One Lord, one faith, one baptism, one God and Father of all, who is above all, and through all, and in you all" (Ephesians 4:3-6). Nothing is lost by agreeing

---

138. *The Evidence of Things Unseen* by Jerry Aveta; P. 69-73; West Bow Press, Bloomington, IN; 2021.

to disagree with the particulars of our faith. Gained is a unified faith of one Spirit in a common identity to accomplish God's purposes.

This is the first challenge to all of us in our pursuit of the common Christian identity of unity. We must choose whether or not our particular beliefs are more important than coming together in our common faith to bring unity to our nation. We must decide if we are trying to impact our nation for God or our particular denomination. I believe when we humble ourselves for the sake of the unity of the church it is a good thing. When we stand on the other side of this life, face to face with our Redeemer, I believe we will get a "Well Done!" Why do I believe that? Because it is exactly what Christ did for us, His church. "Christ also loved the church and gave Himself for it" (Ephesians 5:25); and "He humbled Himself and became obedient to the point of death, even the death of the cross" (Philippians 2:8).

CHRISTIANITY'S COMMON IDENTITY SECOND CHALLENGE: SOCIAL ISSUES

My wife has built several good relationships with a few ladies attending a weekly non-denominational bible study. Subsequently, we have been invited and attended a few Sunday services at one of her friend's churches. One Sunday, an elder in the church invited me to a men's bible study at the church every Thursday morning. I was pleased about the invitation and decided to take him up on it. I found the experience tremendously gratifying and began to attend weekly.

The group of 10-15 men willingly accepted me into their fellowship of faith knowing that I was not a member and that they knew very little about me. I researched the denominational divide of the Presbyterian Church and learned that this church was in the more conservative part of the denomination. It was not long before I had the opportunity to test the willingness of these men to listen to a little different perspective on faith than that of their denomination.

I looked forward to each weekly meeting because this study was open to impromptu discussion that was relative to the topic of the day. Each man was free to speak to edify the learning of the group. In that light, one morning one of the men commented about his concern over their companion denomination's (PCUSA as opposed to the PCA which was hosting the bible study) continued expansion of acceptance of homosexuality.

I took the opportunity to openly discuss my decision to accept two members of my extended family who are openly gay and devout in their Christian faith. One member was in seminary training to be a Jesuit Catholic priest when he openly surrendered to his gay lifestyle. His testimony is that God was with him every step of the way in coming out and his faith is still a vital part of his life. In a recent visit with my other gay family member and her spouse, I asked them where they met. Their answer was "in church." They cultivated a friendship in the fellowship of their church for many months before they started to date. Their faith is still a critical part of their life. After describing both of these relationships I then stated, "I must accept their faith." Then, I asked, "How can I not?" I continued, "I do not have to agree with everything about their faith, but I will not judge it and will accept it as part of my relationship with them." When I asked if they agreed with me, I was greeted with what seemed like a very long silence. Finally, one gentleman asked me "How can you not help but judge them?" I simply responded, "That was above my pay grade."

After a pause, there was a dissenting opinion, using the scriptural reference of Paul's admonition to the Corinthians "not to keep company with sexually immoral people" (1 Corinthians 5:9-11). In that text, Paul goes on to say "not to keep company with" or "eat with" a whole list of other people. This dissenting gentleman went on to advise that not having an association with homosexuals was necessary or else we would be at risk of becoming homosexual ourselves, which he illustrated with a funny face and a "gay-like" greeting. This resulted in a few laughs from some of the other men. He then went on to describe breaking his relationship with his daughter when she went through a stage of rebellion against her faith. She eventually returned to her faith, which in his view was evidence of the wisdom of Paul's directive in the Corinthians reference.

My response was "I very, very respectfully disagree with you." At that point, the discussion moved on to another topic. After the study, I greeted the dissenter, shook his hand, and exchanged pleasantries so there was no ill will from the discussion.

The divide between different views of faith and social issues is difficult to bridge when scriptural arguments are taken out of the context of their writing and used to justify the prejudices that exist in our hearts. In this case, Paul's correction was directed at the hypocrisy of the church's acceptance of a couple that consisted of a young man being with his father's wife. Paul does not elaborate on the details, but it implies a setting similar to a TV soap opera. That is, a son in an inappropriate relationship with his father's wife who is not his mother is quite a scandal and was especially so in those days. It would affect the entire local community of faith. Everyone knows something is wrong, but all willingly turn a blind eye without any leader of the church challenging the situation. That is not the same context as a body of believers willing to accept gay couples into their community of faith. Neither is it the same as dealing with a young adult son or daughter who is struggling with his or her faith. We all struggle with our faith at times. The answer is not to break fellowship with that son or daughter but to stand with that child in love and believe in faith he or she will return to faith as scripture promises (Proverbs 22:6).

Those arguments are so obvious it is hardly worth an open debate if one cannot see the apparent differences in the context. What is even more obvious is the proud prejudice that is hidden in a heart that is revealed when someone openly mocks the gay lifestyle with facial expressions and funny noises to have others join in the mockery. Those antics are not holy nor are they derived from scripture. They reveal a general resistance in the church to accept the faith of people who do not believe exactly as we believe. These are the challenges that must be overcome if we are to attain a common Christian identity concerning social issues.

CHRISTIANITY'S COMMON IDENTITY THIRD CHALLENGE: POLITICS

Today's political environment is probably the most difficult barrier to developing a Christian common identity for two reasons. First, we are experiencing a "monopolization" of our identity by politics. Second, political strategies today are co-oping our faith with a political religion. Both these actions cause a Christian's identity to be dominated by politics more than by one's faith.

First, the "monopolization" of our identity by politics is explained by political scientist Christopher Freiman. He argues that politics is rarely about how we cooperate to solve civic problems and is more about the expression of one's entire identity. Moreover, it is more a defining of ourselves not by whom and what we love but by whom and what we hate. These partisan identities are increasingly anchored to hatred of the opposite party rather than affection for their party. In other words, we hate the other team more than we like our team. That is why not just every election, but every political conversation is so often posed in apocalyptic terms of existential threat.[139]

Developing partisan strategies with a message of hate flows into the flood of disinformation that fills our social media. Hate is a very strong emotion, and a hateful message has a strong impact on its audience. Emotions are not based on facts. Emotions are based on feelings. If you have ever tried to reason someone out of a political position with facts, you probably had a difficult time doing so. That is because many beliefs are more about values than facts. Values are based on what others in our community believe. Our political beliefs become closely held because of the way they make us feel valued by our political community. It is more than what one thinks; it is more about who we believe we are. Our identity becomes rooted in our politics.[140] Many identify themselves as politically "conservative" or "liberal." By doing so, political identities are

---

139. *Why It's OK to Ignore Politics* by Christopher Freiman; P.122; New York: Routledge, 2021.

140. *On Disinformation* by Lee McIntyre; P.96-97; The MIT Press; 2023.

established, and battlelines are mentally drawn. It does not matter what faith we are; political identities take over.

For example, recently there was wide coverage over a stumble our president made while on a trip. Much was said about his inability to walk without being surrounded by help preventing him from falling. That point was made to me in a political discussion with a friend and ended with an emotional question that was delivered very loudly "Is that the kind of president you want?" I was so surprised about the emotion behind the question that the only response I could summon was "What does that have to do with anything?" My point was what did the act of tripping have to do with the ability to lead our nation? I was not surprised that there was no answer given to me by my friend. It was a nonsensical point of discussion that had no basis in fact regarding presidential qualifications. Political arguments often are a result of feelings and emotions that have little to do with facts.

Second, political strategies today co-opt our faith with a political religion. History tells us that political movements, especially authoritarian and totalitarian movements, almost always want to co-opt religion. This is the case with the Chinese Communist Party with Confucianism and the ayatollahs with Islam.[141] In Chapter 11, I described similar efforts ongoing in Russia and even in the Republican Party in our nation today. Beyond that, the political religion that exists today presents a unique challenge to our Christian identity.

David P. Gushee is a Distinguished University Professor of Christian Ethics at Mercer University, Atlanta, Georgia. He also serves as chair of Christian social ethics at Vrije Universiteit and senior research fellow at the International Baptist Theological Study Centre, both in Amsterdam. Gushee has coined the term "Authoritarian Reactionary Christianity" (ARC) as an attempt to name the version of Christian politics that we are experiencing today in our nation that leads to support for or indifference

---

141. *Why It's OK to Ignore Politics* by Christopher Frieman; P.123; New York: Routledge, 2021.

to democratic backsliding.[142] Let's look at each one of these components of Gushee's ARC to understand the blend of faith and politics we are currently experiencing in our nation.

Authoritarianism is the first part of Gushee's term, and it has two components. First is the centralizing power in one person or group, and the second is undercutting free and fair elections.[143] We see both these forms of government actions being enacted today. An example of the first is a recent bipartisan Senate bill proposing control measures for our Southern border that was stopped from consideration in the House of Representatives because of a request from Donald Trump wanting border security to remain an election issue. The second is Donald Trump's efforts to stop our free and fair presidential election in 2021, actions for which he is currently awaiting criminal prosecution. Both these are examples of putting control of the welfare of our country in the hands of one individual and circumventing the democratic process of our government.

Reactionary politics, the second part of Gushee's term, constitutes actions that characteristically involve dramatic changes that evoke equally dramatic reactions against them. These actions represent changes that the overwhelming majority of people are against and typically either block or cause a step back in progress.[144] There is no clearer example of this type of political action than the recent overturning of Roe V. Wade, setting women's abortion rights back decades while a clear majority of the country was against any such action.

Gushee's third term *Christianity* describes a blending of Christian Nationalism and Christian Populism. Christian Nationalism as discussed previously contends that our nation has been and always should be distinctively Christian. Christian Populism is a blend of (1) Trump's promise to Make America Great Again by restoring white Christians to the economic and cultural center of US life and (2) Christian-nation

---

142. *Defending Democracy from its Christian Enemies* by David P. Gushee; P. 43; Wm. B. Eerdmans Publishing Co, Grand Rapids, Michigan, 2023.

143. *Ibid*, P.44

144. *Ibid*, P.49

ideology, which is the belief that America ought to be a white, straight, native-born, hetero-male-led, militarist, authoritarian nation.[145]

Politics is without a doubt the biggest impediment to achieving a common Christian identity of unity. The reason as asserted in the beginning of this section is that our political religion in many cases has taken priority over our common faith. The solution will not be easy, but it is simple. Simple in that it involves only one step. That step is the act for each to humble ourselves to each other for the sake of unity. It is a difficult task because it requires all of us to act together. That can only be achieved by the grace of God. Let me close this chapter with some anecdotal examples, one political and two personal, that perhaps can help illustrate a path forward for us all.

CLOSING THE DIVIDE TO A COMMON CHRISTIAN IDENTITY OF UNITY

The first example of working unified in a common faith is political. A not-so-public fact during the Obama administration was that one of the key advisors in the design and eventual passing of President Obama's Affordable Care Act (ACA, more commonly known as Obamacare) was a Catholic Nun named Sister Carol Keehan. Sister Keehan had a background in nursing and a master's in health care finance, and she served as head of the Catholic Health Association of the United States, which comprises roughly 600 hospitals and 1600 long-term care and other health facilities in all 50 states. Soon after the election of President Obama in November 2008, Sister Keehan and her staff were brought in to help craft the ACA. Sister Keehan explains how she and President Obama, coming from different faith perspectives, were able to merge their efforts into a successful outcome.

"One of our principles was health care is a human right and everybody needs to be in it. We were not getting everybody health care with the ACA. But it didn't violate our principles, because it said that we can take

---

145. *Ibid.*, P.56-57

a giant step forward or we can take no steps. On the other hand, there is the principle of no federal funding of abortion, of euthanasia. And we were very satisfied with that in the bill."[146]

In other words, Sister Keehan was not afraid to compromise in some of her personal doctrinal beliefs of faith for the greater good of providing health care to millions of Americans. That is, she was willing to accept Obamacare as a partial solution to universal health care—partial due to the excepting of funding for abortions and euthanasia. She compromised with her faith in considering a giant step forward in healthcare better than no step at all toward what she believed to be a basic human right for all.

Additionally, I have had two recent experiences with close family members which illustrate the dilemma we are facing with this issue of faith and choice. I was raised Catholic, and many members of my family are still practicing Catholics, some very devout in their faith. A recent discussion with one family member pertained to another family member (deceased for more than 50 years) who had elected to terminate a pregnancy. My relative's doctrinal belief that the punishment for that decision was still ongoing 50 years later for our deceased relative was extremely upsetting to her. I assured her that we cannot know the circumstances affecting her relative's decision, and we cannot possibly comprehend the mind of God. Those arguments did not give her any peace of heart or mind that I could tell, due to her deeply held doctrinal beliefs. A second example involved a relative of mine unleashing a tirade on social media about some comment our president made about a woman's freedom to choose.

Both are examples of how our doctrinal views over the issue of choice create division in communities of faith and families and, in many cases, cause great pain, anger, and frustration to those trying to live by those doctrines. My faith speaks to an understanding of Christ which would not require any follower to feel the hurt, anger, and hateful frustration that my relatives were experiencing because of their doctrinal beliefs over choice. Additionally, my faith speaks to an understanding that my doctrinal beliefs should not trigger such an open display of anger and

---

146. *American Prophets* by Jack Jenkins, P. 18-20, Harper One, 2020.

disrespect for our president. *This is where I draw the line between doctrine and faith. When my belief has to be subject to a doctrine that I can no longer embrace in my heart, I have crossed over from faith to religion. Religion kills faith. Faith breathes spiritual life into our souls.*

Christ was against the religion of the Pharisees. It was the reason He turned over tables in the temple when they had turned a place of worship into a place of enterprise. That is what I feel politics has done to our faith. Those who steer the political machines of our nation have drawn many from the faith communities into the realm of religion in support of a political outcome.

We as people of faith can do better than this. We cannot continue in this same manner. We must embrace the attitude of Sister Keehan and put aside our doctrinal allegiances for the sake of the greater good. We have the freedom of our faith to live in the liberty of the Spirit of God to get along, to compromise, for the greater good. "Where the Spirit of the Lord is, there is liberty" (2 Corinthians 3: 17). Let's use that liberty to come together and resolve our differences in a manner acceptable to all of our faith. Let us find that common ground of faith that we all can embrace. If not, we will retreat into our respective areas of religion, and the divide will grow greater and greater. That is exactly what the politicians want. That was never the plan of Christ.

CHAPTER 13

Seeing One Another

I have spent most of my adult life being color-blind. I never considered it to be a handicap because as a child I was used to the way I saw the world, and no one ever pointed out to me the difference. So, as an adult, I was content and never saw a need to change until one day everything changed. I never saw the world the same way after that day.

My color blindness had nothing to do with the ability of my eyes to distinguish between the spectrum of colors in the world before us. I can now and always have been able to marvel at the colors of a rainbow when it appears after a summer storm. I have been blessed to see the deep blue depths of the ocean and the pristine white snow-capped mountains that are in and around our great nation. My color blindness had nothing to do with the creation of things that we view from afar, but it had everything to do with the created beings that exist right next to us.

On May 25, 2020, an African American man was murdered by a white police officer in Minneapolis, Minnesota, during an arrest made after a store clerk suspected the man may have used a counterfeit $20 bill. The death of George Floyd had an initial dramatic impact on our nation and throughout the entire world. For a seemingly short season, there appeared to be a general awakening to the brutality Blacks have suffered in our nation while under the custody of police. But all too soon things returned to normal. However, watching George Floyd's life seep away while his cries of not being able to breathe were ignored did something to me. Watching the replayed video of a police officer continuing to kneel on the neck of a handcuffed Black man for nine minutes and 29 seconds opened my eyes. For the first time, I was able to "see" the plight of Black people in our nation.

CONDITIONED FOR BLINDNESS

After George Floyd's death, it became apparent to me that I had been conditioned to be blind to color, specifically the color of our nation's Black race, starting from my early days as a youth. Attending a private Catholic elementary school, I cannot remember one Black student in the entire school body during the entire eight years I attended. The only exception was the influx of Cuban refugee girls to the school, mentioned in Part 1 of this book, A few of those girls were assigned to the upper grades. Dark, Spanish-speaking, and somewhat reclusive, these girls were integrated but actually socially isolated. After their initial entry into our white environment, they became largely "unseen" with little to no personal interaction.

My public high school experience was not much different. There were approximately 300 students in my class and 1200 in the whole school. During the four years, I can remember only two Black kids in the entire school, one girl and one boy. The girl was captain of the cheerleaders and one of the most popular girls in school. The boy was a year behind my class and the fastest member of the football team. He was very popular as well. I knew of them but knew nothing about them. They were for the most part "unseen" as part of my high school socialization.

My college class was the first to have Black students in the history of the Virginia Military Institute. One hundred twenty-nine years after the school's founding, five Black students matriculated in my class of 300. One young man shared the same engineering major with me, and we saw each other every day in various classes. We often visited each other's rooms in the cadet barracks and shared the goodies we each got from our home care packages. He was the same to me as any other of my engineering classmates, and soon I did not even "see" that he was Black. Just like all the rest of my casual friends, I knew very little of him personally.

By this time in my life, I was well conditioned to be racially blind. I did not consider myself to be prejudiced, I just was not interested in understanding anything about the plight of the Black race in our nation. At best, I was apathetic toward Black people. Unfortunately, this condition remained in my heart and soul even after I took a deep dive into my faith.

BLINDED BY FAITH

I use the example of a tornado (an unnatural experience) making landfall and changing an entire community (a natural experience) instantly as a metaphor for my faith journey. That is, after a series of intersections between the natural (me) and the supernatural (God), my mind and heart changed instantly. These experiences changed my faith from Catholic to Protestant Christianity, from a non-Pentecostal to a Pentecostal faith, from Baptist to International Pentecostal Holiness denominations, and from church member to church pastor. Each step of the faith journey was initiated and redirected by one of those intersections with God that changed my heart, mind, and faith. But all through that journey, my color blindness persisted. Not openly but in the deep recesses of my heart. I was a good Christian, a good minister, and a good pastor. I was kind and gracious to all members of the church regardless of their skin color. I just didn't "see" everyone until George Floyd's death years after I stopped being a pastor.

I was in a season without church membership preparing to launch my church when I was invited to be part of a local Black congregation. The senior pastor was a neighbor of mine, and we had become friends. When he learned of my desire to start a church, he offered his help and support. He was currently pastoring a thriving church of several hundred members, one that he had started many years earlier. His invitation was for me to be a part of his ministry for a season to learn from his experience, and when the time was right, he would support the launching of my church. He had walked the path that I was about to follow, and he wanted to help by sharing his knowledge of that experience with me.

I was immersed in that Black church community and was only one of two white males in a congregation of several hundred Black men. The men's accountability group was held every Saturday morning at 6:30. Often, it was a time for us to discuss all the frustrations of the week in an open exchange with anyone who wanted to participate. One morning, the discussion turned to the racial tensions and frustrations some of the men were having at work. The discussion went on for some time with a lot of generalities concerning their struggle with "the white man." That phrase was used repeatedly, and often it had a negative connotation. We were sitting in a circle, and I was the only white man present. At first, I thought that some of them were perhaps directing their comments at me for some purpose of discussion, but I soon realized that was not the case.

I believe I had become such a routine part of the group that they no longer "saw" me as white. I was viewed as part of the group regardless of my skin color. At the time, I was flattered by the thought that I had grown so close to these men that race was not an issue. However, I now realize that view is not enough. By not "seeing" someone for who they are, we are not "seeing" them at all. In other words, by not "seeing" someone, I have no great interest in the specifics that distinguish him or her from me. I am subconsciously dismissing their experience as having no relevance or value to me. It amounts to a superficial relationship at best. However, I believe that both sides of my relationship with these men were similar. I felt there was no great interest from my Black brothers in getting to know me, just as I made no effort to get to know them. They never asked my thoughts concerning their struggles with the "white man." What an awful indictment to have about each other as brothers in the faith. What is worse, I now realize I carried that same perspective through all my years of ministry and particularly in my seven years of pastoring.

I had several Black families come and leave my church during my pastoring experience. I believe I served them as a pastor to the best of my ability as I did all in my church. I taught, preached, counseled, and embraced all those in our fellowship of faith equally, without any prejudice in my heart. But I see now I made no effort to get to know any of those Black families other than in a casual way. I did not "see" them personally but just as part of the congregation. I do not believe I am or have ever been a racist. I just was not interested in "seeing" or knowing the context of the racial struggle in our country. I was content as a pastor to not be racially biased, but I had no interest in getting to know any people of color in more than a superficial way. I didn't believe I was a racist, but if this behavior is not racism, what is it?

Bestselling author David Brooks writes,

> The real act of building a friendship or creating a community involves performing a series of small, concrete actions as well: disagreeing without poisoning the relationship; revealing vulnerability at the appropriate pace; being a good listener; knowing how to end a conversation gracefully; knowing how to ask and offer forgiveness; knowing how to let someone down without breaking their heart; knowing how to sit with someone who is suffering; knowing how to host a gathering where everyone feels embraced; knowing how to see things from another's point of view.[147]

Wise counsel for anyone who is interested in building relationships and community in his or her life.

A church is a community of faith built on friendships with trust. As a pastor, I believe I acquired the skills over time to perform all those series of concrete actions described by David Brooks required to build a community. Being respectful, an active listener, forgiving, gracious, and kind are learned behaviors that occupy the mind and heart of an effective

---

147. *How to Know a Person* by David Brooks; P.8; Random House New York; 2023.

pastor. But that last point, knowing how to see things from another's point of view, requires a little something more. The words of that old spiritual hymn (derived from John 9:25) characterize it well: "I once was blind, but now I see." To "see" another person's plight requires something spiritual to happen to change the lens of one's faith. Until that happened to me with the death of George Floyd, you might say I was blinded by my faith. That is, the lens of my faith had not yet adjusted to "see" the plight of Black people in our nation.

"SEEING" IS PERCEIVING

Each of us needs to be recognized as much as we need food and water. To not "see" someone is to render them unimportant or invisible. To do so is to say: You don't matter. You don't exist. No crueler punishment can be devised with such little effort.

There is a scripture referred to in both the Old and New Testaments that gives us some perspective on God's view of "seeing." It is recorded in the gospel of Mathew that Christ is asked by His disciples why He uses parables to teach the crowds that followed Him. In His response, He implies that the crowds were not following Him in any sincere motive of faith but more following the crowd to observe all the action. In other words, they were embracing the excitement of the moment and not the power of His message. He describes those crowds as "seeing they do not see, and hearing they do not hear, nor do they understand" (Mathew 13:13). He goes on as a point of emphasis to His disciples to repeat the words of the prophet Isaiah "Hearing you will hear and shall not understand and *seeing you will see and not perceive*" (Isaiah 6:9). In other words, to "see," one must perceive. That is, to see someone we must attain an awareness or an understanding of that person. Otherwise, we are just glancing and not registering anything in our heart, mind, soul, or spirit about the person who happens to be in our line of sight.

When I saw George Floyd's life taken away with such casualness and indifference, I attained an understanding for the first time of the plight of

Black people in our nation. The countless stories that I have heard on the news of Black lives lost in the custody of law enforcement or at the hands of a vigilante "neighborhood" watch suddenly resonated in my mind, soul, spirit, and I was ashamed over my indifference up to that point of my life. I became aware, I understood, I perceived, and I finally was "seeing" the struggle of Black people in our nation from slavery to the present day.

GOING FROM BLINDNESS TO "SEEING" BY FAITH AND WORK

We are living during an epidemic of blindness in our nation. That is, in the words of Brooks:

> ...we live in an environment in which political animosities, technological dehumanization, and social breakdown undermine connection, strain friendships, erase intimacy, and foster distrust. We're living in the middle of some sort of vast emotional, relational, and spiritual crisis. It is as if people across society have lost the ability to see and understand one another, thus producing a culture that can be brutalizing and isolating.[148]

But all is not lost. "Now faith is the realization of things hoped for, the evidence of things unseen" (Hebrews 11:1). By faith the things that are unseen are realized. If anyone is suffering from not being able to see or perceive or attain understanding or awareness of others it can be accomplished through faith. But faith alone will not do it. Faith requires some sweat equity according to James. Faith without works is dead (James 2:17). Christ in His earthly ministry sometimes required some involvement from those He was healing. John Chapter 9 describes Jesus requiring a blind man to receive healing of restored vision by washing in the nearby pool of Siloam after He had applied a clay pack to the man's eyes made with a little spit. Sometimes, God requires of us some action of

---

148. *Ibid.*, P.97.

faith to receive the outcome of that faith. Such is the case to achieve the miracle of racial reconciliation in our current times. Racism is embedded into our life to such an extent it will require faith with works.

UNITED TOGETHER FOR JESUS (UT4J)

UT4J is a ministry in a local Assembly of God church near where I live. The ministry was birthed out of the pastor's heart for reconciliation between people of different colors in our nation. The vision for the UT4J team at this church is to be a model in its spirit of unity and oneness while celebrating their differences in race, culture, and life experiences for others in and outside the local church community. Their intent is to walk together in their common faith in Christ recognizing their strengths through their diversity. Their desire is to share this learning experience by facilitating the development of similar UT4J teams in other local churches and the local community.

This church community has been on this reconciliation mission for several years at the time of this writing. The result is a core interracial team dedicated to the cause of reconciliation between people of different colors first in the church and then beyond into our nation. It is a labor of love by faith that is desperately needed at this time. I hold up this effort as a model for similar efforts to be launched all over our nation by God's grace, by the faith of God's people, and by the unity of their labor.

But not all racial barriers require a great deal of work to be broken. Some are naturally torn down through the love of one expressed to another regardless of their skin color.

"SEEING" THE LOVE OF A MOTHER FROM ANOTHER

My wife lived on four different continents before she was ten years old. Her father was in the State Department, which took her family from Washington D.C. to Germany to the West Indies to Canada to New Jersey. It was there in New Jersey we met in a high school physics class in the fall of 1967.

When my wife was five years old, she lived in Trinidad because her dad was part of the U.S. diplomatic delegation on the island. A diplomat's lifestyle requires a great deal of socializing with home country officials. Consequently, adequate housing and a staff of servants are provided to host these frequent social functions. A maid, cook, gardener and a nanny to take care of my wife and her younger brother comprised the servant staff. Yvonne Pierre was in her mid-thirties and described as pretty, gracious, and graceful, with a beautiful smile. She was brown skinned with black hair tied neatly behind her head. She was a thin lady with a very traditional look with fine features. She served as my wife's nanny for three years in Trinidad and moved with her to Vancouver, Canada for three more years. Yvonne served as my wife's primary caregiver from the age of five to eleven.

The family moved to Canada without my wife's mother. After living in Canada for two years, it was announced to my wife that her dad and mom were getting a divorce. She was devastated by the news even though her mother had come to visit for only two days during the previous two years in Canada. Approximately a year later, my wife and her brother, escorted by Yvonne, traveled by train from Canada to a remote farmhouse in Stockton, New Jersey to live with her mother. After a day or so, Yvonne said her goodbyes and left. They never talked again.

What was left in my wife's heart was the impression that Black women make wonderful mothers and that Black children are lucky to have a mother that would make them feel so secure. What the child within my wife's heart is saying is that for six years during the critical ages of five through eleven she always felt secure in the love provided by Yvonne. While I am sure that some who attended those diplomatic social events in my wife's home saw a woman of color being paid to take care of two children, what my wife experienced was a woman of color who loved her and her brother like a mother, more present than their actual mother.

There is no virtue greater than love. It supersedes both faith and hope which are pretty great in themselves (1 Corinthians 13:13). There is no greater love than sacrificing oneself for others (John 15:13). Love transcends any racial barrier. All we have to do is love one another. We can't begin to love someone until we "see" them first like Yvonne did.

Yvonne did not "see" two privileged white kids whose parents were too busy or too at odds with one another to take care of them. What Yvonne did "see" were two young souls who were in desperate need of acceptance, security, and love. Yvonne was able to "see" the void in the lives of these children that could only be filled by being present and in the moment day in and day out. In other words, she saw the needs of two children to have at least one parent dedicated to meeting those needs, regardless of their skin color.

We all can learn from Yvonne's legacy that lives on in the heart of my wife. If we can look past the color of each other's skin, we can "see" the need for one another and act on it. I recently was sitting in on a counseling session by a therapist between a mother and her daughter. I heard the therapist ask each one the question "Do you want a relationship with the other, or do you want to just have it your way?" I think that is a worthy question we need to ask ourselves in all our relationships. Do we want a relationship or our way? I think there is a lot of effort being made to get things our way. Let's begin "seeing" one another and pursuing a relationship instead!

CHAPTER 14

Fixing What Is Broken

Dayton, Ohio
August 7, 1865
To My Old Master, Colonel P.H. Anderson, Big Spring, Tennessee

Sir: I got your letter and was glad to find that you had not forgotten Jourdon and that you wanted me to come back and live with you again, promising to do better for me than anybody else can. I have often felt uneasy about you. I thought the Yankees would have hung you before this for harboring Rebs they found at your house. Suppose they never heard about your going to Colonel Martin's to kill the Union soldier that was left by his company in their stable. Although you shot at me twice before I left you, I did not want to hear of your being hurt and am glad you are still living. It would do me good to go back to the dear old home again and see Miss Mary and Miss Martha and Allen, Esther, Green, and Lee. Give my love to them all, and tell them I hope we will meet in the better world, if not in this. I would have gone back to see you all when I was working in the Nashville Hospital, but one of the neighbors told me that Henry intended to shoot me if he ever got the chance.

I want to know particularly what the good chance is you propose to give me. I am doing tolerably well here. I get twenty-five dollars a month, with victuals and clothing; have a comfortable home for Mandy, - the folks call her Mrs. Anderson, - and the children – Milly, Jane, and Grundy – go to school and are learning well. The teacher says Grundy has a head for a preacher. They go to Sunday school, and Mandy and me attend church regularly. We are kindly treated. Sometimes we overhear others saying, "Them colored people were slaves" down in Tennessee. The children feel hurt when they hear such remarks; but I tell them it was no disgrace in Tennessee to belong to Colonel Anderson. Many darkeys would have been proud, as I used to be, to call you master. Now if you will write and say what wages you will give me, I will be better able to decide whether it would be to my advantage to move back again.

As to my freedom, which you say I can have, there is nothing to be gained on that score, as I got my free papers in 1864 from the Provost–Marshall–General of the Department of Nashville. Mandy says she would be afraid to go back without some proof that you were disposed to treat us justly and kindly; and we have concluded to test your sincerity by asking you to send us our wages for the time we served you. This will make us forget and forgive old scores and rely on your justice and friendship in the future. I served you faithfully for thirty-two years, and Mandy twenty years. At twenty-five dollars a month for me, and two dollars a week for Mandy, our earnings would amount to eleven thousand six hundred and eighty dollars. Add to this the interest for the time our wages have been kept back, and deduct what you paid for clothing, and three doctor's visits to me, and pulling a tooth for Mandy, the balance will show what we are in justice entitled to. Please send the money by Adam's Express, the care of V. Winters, Esq., Dayton, Ohio. If you fail to pay us for our faithful labors in the past, we can have little faith in your promises in the future. We trust the good Maker has opened your eyes to the wrongs you and your fathers have done to me and my fathers, in making us toil for you for generations without recompense. Here I draw every Saturday night; but in Tennessee there was never any pay-day for the negroes any more than for the horses and cows. Surely there will be a day of reckoning for those who defraud the laborer of his hire.

In answering this letter, please state if there would be any safety for Milly and Jane, who are now grown up and both good-looking girls. You know how it was with poor Matilda and Catherine. I would rather stay here and starve – and die, if it come to that – than have my girls brought to shame by the violence and the wickedness of their young masters. You will also please state if there has been any schools opened for the colored children in your neighborhood. The great desire of my life is to give my children an education and have them form virtuous habits.

Say howdy to George Carter, and thank him for taking the pistol from you when you were shooting at me.

From your old servant,
Jourdon Anderson[149]

The first time I heard a discussion on reparations my immediate reaction was why should I be liable, I had nothing to do with those atrocities. Jourdan Anderson's letter helps those of us who are generations removed from the acts of slavery understand why the discussion is relevant today. He alludes to the generational impacts when he states, *"We trust the good Maker has opened your eyes to the wrongs you and your fathers have done to me and my fathers, in making us toil for you for generations without recompense."* These atrocities were handed down for generations and inflicted upon generations. It is only through divine revelation to both the sinner and the saint that recompense can be made to the generations still being affected.

MAKING THE CORRECT DIAGNOSIS

Members on both sides of my family have suffered from chronic arthritis. Therefore, it was no surprise to me when I began to suffer from joint pain as I got older. One day playing golf the pain was unusually strong and continually increased while playing. I cut my game short, barely

---

149. Available at https://lettersofnote.com/2012/01/30/to-my-old-master.

able to walk to my vehicle and drive home. Subsequent visits to primary care and orthopedic doctors recommended a diet change along with therapy for knees and back. After several sessions, the therapist began to suspect my issue was not emanating from either the knees or back. It was recommended I see another orthopedic doctor who specialized in hips. It was then I received the recommendation for an immediate double hip replacement. The cause of my pain was improperly diagnosed by several doctors, and I did not take the news well.

Sometimes, we are reluctant to try to fix something if it involves a lot of time, money, and/or effort. Usually, it is easier to buy into the idea if we can address it with an effort that is affordable and can be accommodated by not interrupting our daily routine dramatically. That was the case with my therapy. I was willing to go after work a couple of times a week, and all it cost me was a modest copay for each visit. That was not my reaction to the double hip replacement diagnosis. I went into denial. I delayed taking any action for many months until my condition became so severe it impacted my ability to walk, work, and enjoy a comfortable lifestyle. The life lesson here is to get the proper diagnosis first, then work on the solution quickly because the problem will only worsen.

Fixing a national dilemma that has persisted for generations is not an easy fix. Most important, it requires the correct diagnosis. In other words, fixing something broken requires determining what has to be fixed and how to go about it. The longer one waits before beginning the repair, the more difficult and expensive the repair will be. We have been procrastinating as a nation for generations about the damage done by slavery. It will take a long and costly repair to fix it. More important, it will take a proper diagnosis.

RACISM AND ITS VARIOUS RESPONSES

Racism can be defined as having three elements. First is classifying human beings into distinct "races" due to presumably fixed and hereditary physical characteristics. Second is assigning notions of inferior mental or moral capacities correlating to those physical characteristics. Third, is pushing people who are seen to have those physical, mental, and moral qualities to the margins of a given social order.[150]

In the previous chapter, I talked about the experience of finally "seeing" the plight of the Black people in our nation since the inception of our nation. Recently in a discussion on racism, someone stated that there was only one race: the human race. The implication was that any reference to a race based on color was in itself racist. Unfortunately, those terms have become such a part of our national dialogue that we fall prey to the perception that it is not. Kwon and Thompson note that the first defining element of racism is classifying human beings into distinct races. Doing so does not mean one is a racist in motive and behavior but suggests our thinking is aligned in those general directions. That was my life experience, and I believe it to be the same for many others.

Kwon and Thompson explain:

> When people look at racism, they often see very different things and, further, that these various ways of seeing racism elicit varying responses to it. Some, for example, view racism personally, as a form of personal prejudice whose remedy is personal repentance. Others view it socially, as a form of relational estrangement that requires racial reconciliation. Still, others view it institutionally, in terms of discrete institutional injustice whose redress lies in institutional reform. Each of these accounts holds important truths about the nature of racism and what it means to respond to it fully.[151]

I would have to attest that my view of racism was limited to one of personal prejudice. That is why I could state with all honesty that I was not a racist. I treated all fairly and hid no prejudices in my heart. Now, as a result of "seeing" the issue differently, I do not believe that viewing

---

150. *Reparations, A Christian Call for Repentance and Repair* by Duke L. Kwon and Gregory Thompson; P.14; Brazos Press, 2021.

151. *Ibid.,* P. 14.

racism as personal prejudice is enough. It allows many of us to avoid the problem believing we are not complicit in the offense of racism.

I believe the church struggles with racism. There was a season in the late 1990s when churches were making a concerted effort toward racial reconciliation. The church saw racism as a social issue that was a form of estrangement. I can remember being at a few services where white people were encouraged to reach out to any Black people in attendance and apologize for the social injustices that have gone on in our nation over the years. I can remember thinking I did not understand the purpose. I did no injustice, and I was not prejudiced. I missed the symbolism of acting as part of a national-level reconciliation. Additionally, as there were very few Black people in attendance at the service, it was very easy to avoid participating in any meaningful way by watching others go through the motions of reconciliation.

Recently, the U.S. Supreme Court made a historic decision that effectively ended race-conscious admission programs at colleges and universities across the country. In a divided decision, the court invalidated admissions programs at Harvard and the University of North Carolina. The decision reversed decades of precedent upheld by narrow Supreme Court majorities. It ends the ability of colleges and universities, both public and private, to consider race as one of many factors in deciding which of the qualified applicants is to be admitted.[152]

Affirmative action has been an ongoing effort in our nation starting with President Lyndon Johnson (1963-69) aimed at improving employment and educational opportunities for African Americans while civil rights legislation was passed to dismantle the legal basis for discrimination.[153]

I wrote in Part 1 of this book that civil rights legislation initiated by President Johnson was not renewed by our current Congress. The recent Supreme Court rulings on affirmative action are examples of how our

---

152. "Supreme Court guts affirmative action, effectively ending race conscious admissions" by Nina Totenberg; NPR LAW; June 29, 2023.

153. Britannica; definition of "affirmative action".

nation's response to institutional reform combating racism is in a state of transition, departing from the institutional norms that have been in place for many years in our nation.

It can be said that attempts to combat racism either on a personal level, through the efforts of the church, or via government-sponsored institutional reform have fallen woefully short in combatting racism in our nation. Kwon and Thompson, both pastors deeply involved in various efforts concerning race, equity, and racial repair, believe still another view of racism is required.

THE CASE FOR REPARATIONS

I believe the case for reparations couldn't be made more compellingly than Jourdon Anderson's letter to his former master that opened this chapter. In this former slave's words, we hear the case for reparations articulated even though he never uses those words. He describes not only the material loss suffered by his family but also their greater personal losses of freedom, respectability, physical safety, family unity, self-esteem, gratification, medical care, proper nutrition, education, and hope for the future. They were treated as equals to "horses and cows" in Jourdon's own words. They were left with generational scarring of their children not only being void of any formal education but in physical danger and fear of sexual assault. So much so that Jordan records he "would rather die" than subject his children to that abuse again.

Putting those things aside, if we could, let's talk about the financial loss at stake. Combined, this couple invested 52 years of labor. That is greater than my 30 years of Federal Service, in which I was rewarded with a 55% retirement wage equivalent to the average of my three highest years in salary. Jourdon and his wife labored more than eight hours many days among the hardest, back-breaking labor for which they asked an equivalent wage inflated for the delayed payment minus expenses. Far less than the equivalent cost of 52 years of non-slave labor.

If the Anderson family received all they were asking, it wouldn't have come close to closing the financial, material, and personal losses they had realized over their 52 years of service. The impact of that deficit would also be realized in the future generations of the Anderson family. In other words, the Andersons in the future would be competing on an uneven playing field, always trying to catch up to where the family should be economically.

The best comparison I can think of to illustrate the consequences of slavery in our nation is to use my own family. I am only one generation removed from being an immigrant to this great nation of ours. My grandparents, on both sides of my family, immigrated from Italy in the early 1900s. They lived very humble, modest lives doing various manual labor jobs ranging from working in the coal mines of Pennsylvania to factory work in Philadelphia to chicken farming in New Jersey. My late aunt told me stories of my father and my uncles driving from the farm into the neighborhoods of New York City to sell eggs and slaughtered chickens. My paternal grandfather served in World War I, and my dad and uncles served in World War II. Having survived their respective combat service they went on to establish the foundation of my family that stretches as far west as California and as far south as Florida. None of that would have happened if my grandparents, when they stepped off the boat from Italy, were taken into chattel slavery.

The consequences of any such action as that would have set my family back for generations. I would never have had the opportunity to go to college, to serve my country first in the U.S. Air Force as a commissioned officer and then as a Civil Servant for 30 years. I would never have had the opportunity to go to a seminary and serve in the faith of my choice as a minister and pastor for many years. My grandparents were free to make a life for themselves, my parents, for me, our children, and our children's children.

However, that was not the case for all generations in our nation's history. That was not the case for those who arrived by boat in chains. When we consider dealing with that kind of loss for an entire nation, it requires some fresh thinking and a new approach.

SEVEN CORE CONVICTIONS TO ACHIEVE REPARATIONS

Kwon and Thompson advocate framing the response to racism in our nation around seven core convictions. The first core conviction is simply defined as the nature of racism. The nature of racism is expressed in three parts or steps. *First,* is classifying human beings into distinct "races" due to presumably fixed and hereditary physical characteristics. *Second,* is assigning notions of inferior mental or moral capacities correlated to those physical characteristics. *Third,* pushing people who are seen to have those physical, mental, and moral qualities to the margins of a given social order. [154]

Kwon and Thompson's second core conviction is that "racism is best understood *culturally* as a force that shapes the entire ecosystem of meanings, values, ideas, institutions, and practices of American culture." [155] Seeing racism in this way reminds us that each of us is implicated in and affected by its reality and pervasiveness. The best way to understand the cultural order of racism is through the lens of white supremacy. The white supremacy of today is not represented by the hooded, torch-bearing, cross-carrying marchers in the streets of years past who are memorialized in our collective memory as a nation. It is simply the result of the American social order that benefits those deemed to be white while those not deemed white are enslaved, degraded, and marginalized.

The third conviction views white supremacy to be a multigenerational campaign of cultural theft, in which the identities, agency, and prosperity of African Americans are systematically stolen and given to others. This includes the theft of truth, the theft of power, and the theft of wealth. [156]

The fourth conviction is that the Christian church in America has a fundamental responsibility to respond to the theft experienced by African Americans. This is found in the many scriptural mandates related to faith and liberty similar to and including verses like the words of Jesus

---

154. *Reparations, A Christian Call for Repentance and Repair* by Duke L. Kwon and Gregory Thompson; P.14; Brazos Press, 2021.

155. *Ibid.,* P.15

156. *Ibid.,* P.16

to "proclaim the good news to the poor" and "liberty to the captives" (Luke 4:18).[157]

The fifth conviction is that there is a long scriptural and deep theological tradition in the Christian church which teaches that when you take something that does not belong to you, love requires you to return it. This is the church's historic ethic of culpability and restitution.[158]

Similarly, the sixth conviction is that the Christian Church also teaches that restoration is another response to theft. Even when not culpable for a theft, the Christian still should restore what was lost as seen in the story of the good Samaritan. "These two ethical responses to theft—restitution where we are culpable and restoration even when we are not—provide a broad foundation for a Christian account of reparations."[159]

The seventh conviction is that as the church undertakes the work of reparations, it must mirror the threefold theft wrought by White supremacy, theft of wealth, truth, and power.[160]

I do not have the experience nor the depth of understanding that Pastors Kwon and Thompson have when it comes to the social implications of a subject like reparations. Nonetheless, I have independently come to some of the same general conclusions.

I agree that the solution to the social divide in our nation has to come from the Church. I also agree the Church is complicit in causing division in our nation because the Church is so divided. I thoroughly agree with the Church's mandates of restitution and restoration. I also understand the association between racism and white supremacy; however, being a white person who does not believe in white supremacy and, to the best of my knowledge, never personally practiced it, I find difficulty embracing that association. That sensitivity is addressed by Kwon and Thompson: "Another difficulty some might have with the language of

---

157. *Ibid.*, P.17.
158. *Ibid.*, P.17.
159. *Ibid.*, P.17.
160. *Ibid.*, P.18.

White supremacy regards not necessarily what it means but how it feels." They go on to explain although it sounds offensive, not to express it in those terms will in essence perpetuate the logic of white supremacy. That is, if racism is defined as giving advantages to white people and putting non-white people at a disadvantage, Kwon and Thompson then ask, "What other term does honesty permit us to use?"[161]

I must admit it is hard to argue with that logic, given the scope of racism as they have defined it: putting people of color at a disadvantage for the entire American ecosystem of meanings, values, ideas, institutions, and practices of culture. There is no better description than "white supremacy" which characterizes the complete advantage and total dominance of one person compared to another.

Kwon and Thompson provide corroboration in great detail that the implementation of reparations is not a simple or easy task. I do not have the ability or space in this writing to summarize the extent of their recommendations. I will simply summarize their effort describing the action as three different calls. They are the call to "See," "Own," and "Repair." Of course, implicit in their convictions the call is made to the Church. The Church must lead the way. Why? Because the Church is to bear the light. "Then Jesus spoke to them again, saying, *I am the light of the world. He who follows Me shall not walk in darkness but have the light of life* (John 8:12)."

That being said, Kwon and Thompson do not consider the Church alone to be responsible (or, for that matter, even capable) of doing all the work necessary to implement reparations. Rather, it can only be a collaboration between many groups. They note a historical disparity among these groups: "…some Christian communities—especially African American churches—have long labored toward the work of reparations, even as other churches have labored against it."[162]

---

161. *Reparations, A Christian Call for Repentance and Repair* by Duke L. Kwon and Gregory Thompson; P.16; Brazos Press, 2021.

162. *Ibid.,* P. 18.

However, their premise on the subject remains as mine: the effort should start with the Church. That does not mean the Church can or will do all the work required, but the Church should be facilitating conversation. It has become painfully obvious to me that most churches that I have attended regularly do not discuss these issues. It is not even on the list of topics to be discussed. That is because most church members do not "see" the problem even though it persists all around us. People are not walking around in chains that we can see. They are walking around bound by being disenfranchised from life's competition. They never got a shot at a good start. They entered life's competitive race a few laps behind.

Let me emphasize that while I believe the church should lead the way to reparations, it will take more than the church community to implement reparations throughout our nation. All communities must embrace the responsibility to eliminate the toxic poison of racism that permeates our nation.

THE DISENFRANCHISED ARE ALL AROUND US

Chattel slavery has been abolished from the daily experience of our nation. Our constitution guarantees it will never return to our land, but the shadows of chattel slavery still exist all around us. Even though there are no cotton fields being worked by slave labor and no other obvious demonstrations of an enslaved life, the shadows of that life are all around us. Those people who have been cheated out of a fair start work in the kitchens of the restaurants where we dine. They clean our children's schools at night. They groom the fairways and manicure the greens at our golf clubs. If they happen to pass within our view, we hardly see them.

I am not sure how my relationship with Randy (not his real name) started. I believe it began with a wave and a casual comment like "Beautiful day, isn't it?" Before we realized it, my wife and I began to look for Randy whenever we played a round of golf at our local club. As our interactions grew, we learned more about his life, his work, and a little about his family. We learned he liked to grill chicken when he could at his home, and it was his family's favorite.

I include Randy as one of those "disenfranchised" who are all around us. We never had a discussion of his family history, but there was evidence both in his appearance and in our discussions that led us to believe it been poor. First was the smile that was always on his face whenever we talked. He is a happy soul and not at all concerned that his smile reveals his missing teeth. It never bothered us as well. When asked if he had always done this kind of work, he willingly disclosed his happiness to be out of the hot kitchens where he used to work. He prefers the pristine environment of a golf course even on hot days.

There was no remorse in Randy's discourse concerning limited career choices that day or any day we talked. Even on the rare occasion when we see hm driving through our little local town in his truck smiling and waving as he passes there is no indication of dissatisfaction with how his life turned out. But I can't help wondering how far he may have gone in life with a little better start. I have no idea of his family history. It doesn't matter if there is a direct link in his inheritance to slavery. The consequences of that period of our nation's history and the ushering in of the racial prejudice that followed have had broad implications to many of color in our nation. Once we start "seeing" the implications of those years, we can start "owning" the problem and then begin the "repair." It begins with "seeing" all those like Randy who are around us every day.

CHAPTER 15

Finding Liberty

Liberty means different things to different people at different times of their lives. In other words, liberty has context. Liberty for those serving in the Armed Services of our country means vacation time away from their duty station. It may mean being off duty for a few hours, or a few days, or a few weeks. Liberty for a young child may mean summer vacation from school. Their joy of freedom is captured in song on the last day ... "No more school, no more books, no more teachers' dirty looks!" When one is given the liberty to speak, it generally means the freedom to say whatever is on their mind at the time. To a person of Christian faith, liberty is the freedom received from a life of faith in Christ (Luke 4:18). That is, the freedom to live from the control of those besetting issues that sometimes enslave us. For some, it may be alcoholism, anger, or depression. Regardless of the entrapment, having faith in a Person, a Power, or a Force beyond our comprehension leads us to a new life of freedom. People of other faiths believe differently. That is liberty.

But liberty concerning our nation has a different context. Our Constitution describes it as "the Blessings of Liberty to ourselves and our Posterity." If we follow the governing principles as described in our

Constitution, we and our descendants will be the recipients of a divinely appointed freedom of living referred to as liberty. A liberty that provides freedom to pursue opportunities for life and living as we choose. It is clear from this Constitutional language that it was the intent of our founding fathers for all who live within the boundaries of our nation to experience that liberty. However, if there is still some doubt, read the Declaration of Independence. It was signed by the Second Continental Congress on July 4, 1776, and it states, "We hold these truths to be self-evident, that all men are created equal, that they are endowed by their Creator with certain unalienable Rights, that among these are Life, *Liberty* and the Pursuit of Happiness."

However, despite our nation's formal declarations of independence and claiming liberty as a fundamental byproduct of its governing constitution, we still seek liberty for all in our nation today. In the entirety of our nation's history, we have never been able to embrace liberty for all within our boundaries. The toxic blend of faith and politics has inhibited the progress of liberty since before the birth of our democracy. That toxic blend provided the acceptance of chattel slavery that robbed our nation of the chance of achieving liberty for all. The danger of an evil like slavery is the ability to disguise itself. In that instance, our nation conducted a war against itself in an attempt to eliminate chattel slavery and provide liberty for all only to find on the other side of that war that the evils of slavery still existed, just in different forms expressed through racism, white supremacy, and low-wage jobs. Now, after decades of fighting for equal rights and liberty for all within the social structure of our nation, we find ourselves losing ground in that battle again. It is a two-front battle of both politics and faith. Both are complicit. Both are the reason that our efforts to attain liberty for all must continue in our nation today. In essence, we are still engaged in the task of finding liberty.

THE EXISTENTIAL THREAT TO LIBERTY TODAY

Faith and politics have converged at the highest levels of our government and some faith denominations. This is an existential threat to our nation's liberty. The blending of faith and politics at the highest levels of our nation, both sacred and secular, permits that toxicity to permeate throughout the nation unabated. The result produces an uneasiness which has been a characteristic of our times. It is a result of a close alignment with the beliefs of some of our faith denominations with politics, so much that in some cases they are inseparable. Let's begin with a quote from a sitting U.S. senator to further describe this existential threat.

Tim Scott has served as the junior United States senator from South Carolina since his appointment in 2013. He stated,

> While the church has historically been a catalyst for positive social and political change, in recent years we've begun to lose our moral and spiritual authority. Instead of bringing the love of Christ into politics, we've let politics affect our love for one another. Is it any wonder, then, that one of the most cited reasons pastors leave the ministry is current political divisions? Nothing and no one are immune from the impact of politics done wrong; not friendships, workplaces, communities, families, or churches—all have been negatively impacted.[163]

I agree with Senator Scott's point that no one is immune from the impact of politics, especially if done wrong. It does not matter how much one follows the events on Capitol Hill or in the White House, the decisions made in those places impact everyone in our nation. I also agree that our love of a preferred political party has affected the love of our faith, but perhaps one comment of Senator Scott that gives me the greatest concern is that politics is the most cited reason for pastors leaving the ministry. That one comment gives us an idea of the pervasiveness of the problem. However, that concern is expressed not only by a sitting member of our Congress but by many contemporary faith leaders like Russell Moore as discussed in chapter six of this book. Another contemporary faith leader speaking out is Jim Wallis.

---

163. *Politics for People Who Hate Politics* by Denise Grace Gitsham; P.11; Bethany House publishers, 2023.

Jim Wallis, the Director of Georgetown University's Center on Faith and Justice, served on President Obama's first White House Advisory Council on Faith-based and Neighborhood Partnerships. In writing about a recent discussion he held with a group of racially diverse pastors following a lecture at the Chandler School of Theology at Emory University concerning the rise of white Christian nationalism in our country, he describes faith as being directly politicized in many white evangelical circles. In some cases, congregational members who didn't share a right-wing partisan agenda are being told to leave.

Wallis discusses these pastoral conversations at length over a number of topics. He describes Black pastors talking about their fears over the rise of white Christian nationalism in churches. White pastors openly talked how truth-telling in mainline denominations about race was increasingly met with aggressive resistance from many white congregants. They shared stories about pastors under attack for honest and healing talk about race. They talked about colleagues losing their jobs and getting death threats. They felt overwhelmed by the barrage of Cable news channels, right-wing radio, and conspiratorial webcasts. All the while they were being told by senior pastors to respect the demographics of top donors. Black pastors were challenging white pastors to tell the truth about our country's racial history to help the country grow into a genuine multiracial democracy. But white pastors were reluctant to do so counting the cost of implicating their careers and their family's welfare.

The existential threat to our nation is illustrated in Wallis' comments by the political pressure pastors are receiving in their churches and their denominations. However, the political pressure on pastors is emanating from the pews due to the influences of social media. Denominational leadership suggests in some cases avoiding confrontation and not antagonizing the status quo. It is easy to criticize denominational faith leaders and pastors for not taking a stand against these political influences when we are not the ones taking the risk of losing an income or a career that we have spent our lives preparing to do. I can attest to having similar concerns when I elected to continue my Federal Career even though I had a strong desire to serve God. The one time I was considered for a full-time ministry position at a local church did not materialize. I am sure if offered the position I would have left Civil Service and served for a fraction of my income at the time. Looking back on that experience, I realize now that would have been a disaster for me and my family. The financial pressures and concerns about providing for the family must be increasingly more difficult for pastors and ministers today. Additionally, these are complex times because the toxic blend of faith and politics is producing a new type of political/denominational church as follows. Grisham (2023) writes

> Most Christians in America choose to attend churches with people who look, talk, and think just like them. They also choose churches that align with their political affiliations. This reality emboldens some pastors to openly endorse candidates from the pulpit, an act that not only jeopardizes their nonprofit tax status, but also distracts from the reason we're there in the first place: to learn about the Only One who can save our nation and our souls.[164]

I have no doubt that some pastors have succumbed to the political pressures they are sensing within their own congregations. I have not witnessed such conduct in the several churches I have attended in recent years. My experience has shown that most pastors steer far away from politics and its effect on the church. Federal regulations have been in place since 1954 prohibiting churches from engaging in any political campaign activity. However, the failure to address this toxic issue in the church has only increased the problem to being the existential threat it is today. It is rapidly accelerating division in the church and causing it to be less effective to its true cause and its influence.

We have been lured into a political fight that includes our faith. Consequently, that blending of faith and politics has left us confused, unfocused, and divided as a nation. The confluence of faith and politics is a toxic blend that distorts our political perspective and dilutes our

---

164. *Politics for People Who Hate Politics* by Denise Grace Gitsham; P.218; Bethany House publishers, 2023.

faith. The consequence of these two reactions results in an inability to compromise. We are backed into our respective corners, secure in our political choices, hiding behind our respective shields of faith preventing any consideration of compromise for the greater good of our nation.

This is not a unique circumstance for our nation or the Christian faith. As mentioned, we find that experience at the origins of our nation. But also, we find a similar partnering of the religious leaders with the political powers at the origins of the Christian faith. There were no recorded doctrines of faith available to guide those first disciples of Christ through the confluence of faith and politics of their time. They ultimately decided to push politics aside and do what was best for the greater good of their newfound faith.

POLITICS, FAITH, AND THE APOSTLES

Mathew's gospel describes the confluence of faith and politics resulting in the crucifixion of Christ. The high priest and the governing leaders of the Jews in Jerusalem convicted Christ of blasphemy because of His claim to being the Son of God and therefore deserving of death (Mathew 26:59-66). Having no ability to execute their sentence on Christ, they turned to the political leader of their times, Pontius Pilate, who acceded to the priest's request and substituted Christ for a convicted criminal (Barabbas) worthy of crucifixion (Mathew 27:22-26).

The toxic blend of faith and politics resulted in Christ's crucifixion. The misguided actions of the faith leaders of those times consorted with the political powers of the day to bring about the desired result for their faith community. The actions taken by these faith leaders were intended to control the faith community under their rule and suppress any notion of a different understanding of faith from that which they taught. They hoped to put an end to this movement headed by the perceived insurrectionist named Jesus Christ whom they intended to murder as soon as possible. After all, they intended to honor the upcoming Passover. They had a religion to protect.

The motivation of the political leader of the times was to keep civil peace. Nothing is more obvious of a political leader's inability to effectively lead his constituency than civil unrest. The last thing Pilate needed was for word to get back to Rome about riots in the streets of Jerusalem. The best political outcome was to end this upheaval quickly. The quickest solution was to kill Christ. He could read the crowd. He had the means to satisfy their bloodlust. He knew it would be easy to work the crowd and produce the desired results of Christ's condemnation without sharing the blame. He could easily "wash his hands" of the entire event and satisfy Roman law. Pilate was a skilled politician.

In other words, the current faith leaders had the intent of eliminating any interpretation of faith other than the one they believed to be true and accurate. They wanted to eliminate the liberty to believe differently from the way they believed. Any action to suppress faith will likely result in resistance and the emboldening of that faith. In this case, the attempted suppression divided the Jewish faith and spawned Christianity and a new liberty in the expression of that faith.

This same intertwining of faith and politics has been going on in our own nation for many years. Some religious leaders have partnered with politicians with the purpose of restricting religious liberties. The goal of those denominational leaders is to bring *all* people of faith into conformity with their particular views of faith. In so doing, they are filling the role of the Pharisees during the times of Christ. The results are taking root and putting our democracy at risk. Let's learn from the example of the Christian church in its beginning how to react to this confluence of faith and politics.

THE RESPONSE OF THE APOSTLES

After Christ's ministry on earth ended, the disciples were left without any written guidance, rules to follow, or any hope of hearing from the One who had directed their way for many months. Pilate was still in charge of the local governance. The High Priest and the Pharisees were still in control of the local faith community of Jews. The apostles were left divided, confused, fearful, and hiding for their lives. All they knew was that they may be next to be hunted down and executed. They were left to make their way through the toxic blend of faith and politics of their times.

The apostles had often heard Jesus teach that the Kingdom of God was nearby. When they witnessed His ascension, it was announced that He would descend from heaven in the same way He ascended (Acts 1:11). Logically, they may have expected His return to be sometime during their lifetime. It is also logical that as the apostles got older, they began to think differently. That is, they began to think that perhaps Christ's return was not as imminent as they had initially thought. As they began to face their own mortality, they began recording the history of their experience through the writing of the gospels. The first gospel was written by Mark sometime past mid-century, followed by Mathew's and Luke's gospels late in the century. Finally, the last gospel written was John's at the turn of the first century. This new season of the apostle's faith was responsible for the written record of Christ's ministry on earth which has been distributed throughout the world for 2,000 years. Their efforts during this new season of faith introduced Christianity to the world.

Jon Meacham writes,

> In writing the gospels, and then in formulating church doctrine in the second, third, and fourth centuries, Jesus's followers reacted to his failure to return by reinterpreting their theological views in light of their historical experience. If the kind of kingdom they had so long expected was not at hand, then Jesus's life, death, and resurrection must have meant something different. The Christ they had looked for in the beginning was not the Christ they had come to know. His kingdom was not literally arriving, but he had, they came to believe, created something new: the Church, the sacraments, the promise of salvation at the last day—whenever that might be.[165]

---

165. *The Hope of Glory* by Jon Meacham; P.23; Convergent Books, 2020.

In other words, given time to reflect on their experiences, the disciples were able to rethink their theology to fit their experience. Christ's return and the new Kingdom were not going to be in place in their lifetime, so they were then able to redefine the significance of their experiences. Their answers were the Church, the people, and the promises of their newfound faith.

The shift of emphasis from the short to the long term was an essential achievement. Because the early believers became convinced that Jesus's Passion and resurrection had given them the keys to heaven, they cared less about the hour of his coming, for God was worth the wait.[166]

In other words, the apostles developed a new approach to their faith. Everything they learned from and by Christ's teachings was still valid. They still had the passion of heart to carry out Christ's mandate of spreading the word of their newfound faith, but because of their experience, they had to reshape their approach. They had to change their focus to help the people of their time understand the confusion of the day as a result of the blending of faith and politics.

Those who walked with Christ during His earthly ministry listened to His teachings, witnessed His miracles, and were closest to Him, but they still couldn't initially figure out how to integrate their faith into the current circumstances. It took time to digest their experiences and make the required adjustments to align their faith with the present. It required a new revelation of the same faith. They were finally able to see through the confusion of the blending of faith and politics to see God's purposes through their circumstances. Their theological view shifted from a focus on the final goal of their faith to a focus on the present circumstances moving forward in their faith. They were initially preoccupied with the establishment of the eternal rule of the Kingdom of God even without a clear understanding of exactly how and when that would occur. Now they came to realize that their real purpose was to deal with the circumstances of their times and prepare the people of faith for living through them.

---

166. *Ibid.*, P.23.

Here is the lesson for us. If the disciples of Christ can change their theology based on their experiences, so can we. Given time and experience, we, too, can shift our emphasis to see God's purposes through the haze of the blend of faith and politics of our times. We, too, must shift the focus from the establishing of the expected outcomes of our faith to navigating our faith through the present malaise caused by the blending of faith and politics. We, too, are in a time that requires a new season of our faith. This new season first requires a new view or a new approach to our faith. I believe this new view will give us new revelation to see through the malaise of our times. This revelation requires us to see through the turbulence and then take our first step with a clear view. Before we renew our quest of "finding liberty," however, we have to know what we are looking for. In other words, how will we recognize liberty in this toxic environment of faith and politics? I think it has to begin with an open and honest discussion about our faith.

FREE TO TALK ABOUT FAITH

I recently had an overnight hospitalization after a surgical procedure. The night shift, which ran roughly from 7 p.m. to 7 a.m., was staffed by a nursing assistant of Asian descent who had immigrated here many years ago. She would come into my room periodically to check and record all the necessary information monitoring my recovery from the surgery. I am not sure when or how our casual discussions concerning faith started, but I am sure she was the one to introduce the subject. I tried not to encourage the conversation at first, not sure of her motives, and I was in no mood to be evangelized. After a few minutes, I realized her conversation was an outflow of her daily life experience of her faith. She got great joy talking about her faith without any attempt to influence me at all. At that point, I embraced the opportunity, started asking her questions, and learned she was a Buddhist. I shared a little about myself and mentioned I enjoyed writing about my faith. At that point, she began to act like I was some famous movie star!

Our first conversation went on so long that she became tardy in completing her rounds. For the rest of the evening, she would duck into my room and talk for a few minutes. She was so thrilled to talk to someone about faith and spiritual issues. We talked about both the differences and the commonalities of the two faiths, neither threatening nor judging the other's faith. Both of us enjoyed the liberty we had discussing our faith with one another. Before she went off duty, she came and asked for information on how to buy my books. I offered to send her some copies when I was released from the hospital. When she received them, she sent me a very kind note thanking me and promising she would enjoy reading them!

The point of the story is to answer the question of how we will know liberty when we see it. The answer is we will know it when we see it in others! When we see others acting out liberty in our discourse, our interrelationship, and our life experiences, then we are truly in the presence of liberty. Why does it have to begin with a discussion about faith? It is because I believe we "evangelical" Christians have become so entrenched in our doctrinal beliefs that we have closed ourselves off to an open discourse about faith without trying to convince everyone of faith to believe exactly as we do. I learned this to be true as I experienced my faith journey across four different denominations within the Christian faith. I think we have begun to act a little like the Pharisees during the first-century Church trying to constrain all to believe the same way.

I believe this ability to openly discuss faith and acknowledge other beliefs as acceptable is critical to "finding liberty" in our nation again. The existential threat due to the toxic blending of faith and politics has left a web of complex issues entangled in the individual social relationships in our nation today. To begin a complex discussion, we must first begin a conversation about faith to establish a common ground in one of the two blended topics. We must start our discussion with our faith because we have more in common with our faith than we do differences. All we have to do is agree to disagree on our doctrinal differences. I believe when we all get to the other side of this life and are in the presence of God, our doctrinal differences will not matter. Once we establish a discourse of faith without judgment for believing differently, then we can move on to the challenge of reconciling our politics through our faith. Again, the goal is to agree to disagree on our political differences. The object is to heal the relational divide, not convert anyone's political allegiance.

This cannot be a top-down approach for two reasons. First, the partnering of some denominational leaders of the church with the political leaders of our nation began years ago. Recently those bonds have been reinforced with the advocation of Christian Nationalism in the highest levels of our government. Therefore, any effort to mitigate this toxic blend of politics and faith must be initiated from the bottom to the top beginning in the lives of the church members. Second, social media is driving the political pressure on pastors through the members of the local church. The object is to confront the issue at the source of the pressure: church membership. However, many churches are political minefields. Any political discourse should proceed cautiously to avoid any detonation of emotion. One must strive to be familiar with the nature of the church's political landscape before venturing into any political discussions.

The Church reflects today's polarization between Republican and Democrat, between red and blue. Each party's activist base, in fact, is rooted in an expression of the Church. Recent polls confirm that upwards of 80% of congregants in certain denominations belong to the same political party.[167] This explains how some Christians grow so extreme in their beliefs. It's nearly impossible not to conform when everyone around you asserts that the only godly way of thinking is theirs."[168]

---

167. *U.S. Religious Groups and Their Political Leanings* by Michael Lipka; pew Research Center, February 23, 2016.

168. *Politics for People Who Hate Politics* by Denise Grace Gitsham; P.219; Bethany House publishers, 2023.

"FINDING LIBERTY" THROUGH GRACE

The late Bishop Carlton D. Pearson has been quoted as having said "If I am judged for perceiving Christ or Christianity in error, I'd rather be wrong for overestimating the love of God than underestimating it. I'd rather err on the goodness, greatness, and graciousness of God than the opposite." Bishop Pearson's story about his fall from denominational grace has been well documented in the 2018 film "Come Sunday." He walked away from a very successful church and ministry as the result of a revelation concerning a denominational doctrine that he could no longer accept as part of his faith. Many described his new faith position as too liberal. I call it finding liberty in one's faith.

Finding liberty must first occur in the eye of the beholder. That is, if I view a person like Bishop Pearson and label him in my heart as a liberal, a heretic, or just a nut, I am only imprisoning myself. My views do not affect the person I am judging; they remain free in their liberty. I am imprisoned in my judgment. That is because when it comes to faith, there is an interrelationship between liberty and grace. To embrace liberty in our faith, we must employ grace. Being dogmatic, critical, and judgmental of another's faith removes grace from the environment of our hearts and weakens our faith.

The only reason any of us can enter into the Christian faith is because of the grace of God. Ephesians 2:8 describes Christ's redemptive work for us, the cornerstone of our faith, as a gift from God by His grace. In other words, grace is an inherent part of our faith relationship. We would not have faith without grace. They are opposite sides of the same faith coin commodity. So, there is a spiritual dynamic between faith and grace. There is a similar spiritual dynamic between faith and liberty.

Christ's redemptive work is the foundation that frees us into a new life of faith. The product of our faith is liberty. Galatians 5:1 describes we are to "stand fast in the liberty by which Christ has made us free." Our faith produces liberty which we are to strive to maintain.

Putting these two spiritual dynamics together, we have grace-producing faith which produces liberty. To understand how these three elements work together, let us imagine a balance scale with trays on either side used to measure weight or mass of an object. In order to have a balanced life of faith, we must have equal measures of grace and liberty. Having no grace leads to a faith full of restrictions and little liberty. Having no liberty is a result of a faith with little grace.

GRACE IS THE SALT FOR A POLITICAL DISCUSSION

Any discussion involving faith and politics has the likelihood at any point during the discussion of becoming emotional and/or defensive. Even starting a conversation about either of these subjects is difficult to do without arousing some of those same emotions. How does one manage to have a reasonable discussion with topics that seem so unreasonable at times? Scripture gives us some insight on how to approach such a situation.

First, we are to approach anyone that we perceive may believe differently, in this case either in faith and/or politics, "with wisdom redeeming the time" (Colossians 4:5). That is, simply put, we are to conduct our conversation in such a way that these same folks would be willing to talk again soon.

Second, the way we achieve that first result is by seasoning our conversation with grace, like adding salt to adjust a recipe, to adjust our conversation in a manner that will be acceptable (Colossians 4:6). Jim Wallis suggests setting the stage for such discussions with questions that will set the tone as seeking information rather than advocating a particular position. For example:

- Where do you get your news and what other sources might prove helpful when trying to navigate these challenging issues?

- How and where can we find more truthful information and perspectives on things?

- Instead of going further right or left, how might you go deeper and what would that look like for you? Remember we are seeking information, not ammunition to prove anyone is right or wrong.[169]

Additionally, Wallis suggests the following approach:

- Identify someone in your friend group with whom you disagree.

- Offer to only listen to their views as a way to build equity and establish trust.

- During the conversation, look for common ground:
    - What do we agree upon?
    - What personal and faith values do we share?"[170]

SOME FINAL THOUGHTS ON "FINDING LIBERTY"

In 2008, pastor, teacher, and author Timothy Keller wrote the following words in his introduction to his latest book, at the time entitled *The Reason for God*. He states, "There is a great gulf today between what is popularly known as liberalism and conservatism. Each side demands that you not only disagree with but disdain the other as (at best) crazy or (at worst) evil. This is particularly true when religion is the point at issue."[171]

Those words seem to describe a toxic blend of faith and politics much like what we are experiencing today. The truth of the matter is that this challenge has been a part of our nation for many years. Unfortunately, in 2008 many like me were unaware of the toxic blend of faith and politics permeating our nation at the time. We were busy making a living, raising a family, being actively involved in our faith, and only paying casual interest now and then to politics. The result is an existential threat to our democracy today. The replacement of our democracy with a form of

169. *The False White Gospel– Rejecting Christian Nationalism, Reclaiming True Faith, and Reforming Democracy* by Jim Wallis, P. 245, St. Martin's Publishing Group, 2024.

170. *Ibid.*, P. 245, St. Martin's Publishing Group, 2024.

171. *The Reason for God – Belief in an Age of Skepticism* by Timothy Keller; P. ix, Penguin Group, 2008.

autocratic government may result from the 2024 presidential election. I hope to contribute to mitigating the chances of that possibility in some small way with the publication of this writing.

Nonetheless, I have no regret for the hours spent pecking at the keyboard of my laptop or in endless discussion with my wife as we partnered to say things in a meaningful way because this is such a critical time in our nation we were compelled to act. And in that action, as we pursued to communicate about the necessity to preserve the liberties to our faith and our politics, we found our own personal liberties. We were able to define in our own hearts and minds what liberty means to us, what it looks like in our view, and how to go about maintaining it in our own lives.

We hope that readers of this book will have the same positive experience, that they, too, will find liberty in their faith and politics. More than anything, we hope that our research, discoveries, and efforts will be able to guide those who read this book through the turmoil and past the instinctive hatred of the other that has been created by the current toxic blend of faith and politics! And we pray for the day that the toxicity becomes part of history, neither characteristic of the present moment nor boding ill for the future.

Other Books by Jerry Aveta

Faith for the Times: From the Shadows into the Marvelous Light

The Evidence of Things Unseen: Faith Revealed in a Family, in a Community and a Nation

MSI Press LLC
Publications in Religion
and Philosophy

A Believer-in-Waiting's First Encounters with God (Mahlou)

A Guide to Bliss: Transforming Your Life through Mind Expansion (Tubali)

A Theology for the Rest of Us (Yavelberg)

An Afternoon's Dictation (Greenebaum)

Blest Atheist (Mahlou)

Christmas at the Mission: A Cat's View of Catholic Beliefs and Customs (Sula)

Easter at the Mission: A Cat's Observation of the Paschal Mystery (Sula)

Dia de Muertos (Sula)

El Poder de lo Transpersonal (Ustman)

Everybody's Little Book of Everyday Prayers (MacGregor)

God Speaks into Darkness (Easterling)

GodSway (Keathley)

Good Blood (Schaffer)

Heart to Heart Resuscitation (Montgomery)

How to Argue with an Atheist: How to Win the Argument without Losing the Person (Brink)

How to Live from Your Heart (Hucknall)

Introductory Lectures on Religious Philosophy (Sabzevary)

Jesus Is Still Passing By (Easterling)/Study Guide edition also available

Joshuanism (Tosto)

Lamentations of the Heart (Wells-Smith)

Life after Losing a Child (Young & Romer)

Living in Blue Sky Mind: Basic Buddhist Teachings for a Happy Life (Diedrichs)

Of God, Rattlesnakes, and Okra (Easterling)

One Family: Indivisible (Greenebaum)

Overcoming the Odds (C. Leaver)

Passing On (Romer)

Puertas a la Eternidad (Ustman)

Rainstorm of Tomorrow (Dong)

Road Map to Power (Husain & Husain)

Saints I know (Sula)

Seeking Balance in an Unbalanced Time (Greenebaum)

Since Sinai (Gonyou)

Sula and the Franciscan Sisters (Sula)

Surviving Cancer, Healing People: One Cat's Story (Sula)

Surviving Freshman Year (Jones)

Tale of a Mission Cat (Sula)

The Rise and Fall of Muslim Civil Society (O. Imady)

The Seven Wisdoms of Life (Tubali)

Weekly Soul (Craigie)

When Liberty Enslaves (Aveta)

When You're Shoved from the Right, Look to Your Left: Metaphors of Islamic Humanism (O. Imady)

www.ingramcontent.com/pod-product-compliance
Lightning Source LLC
Chambersburg PA
CBHW062211270326
41930CB00009B/1711